ClearRevise

AQA GCSE
English Literature

Illustrated revision and practice

Macbeth
By William Shakespeare

Published by
PG Online Limited
The Old Coach House
35 Main Road
Tolpuddle
Dorset
DT2 7EW
United Kingdom

sales@pgonline.co.uk
www.clearrevise.com
www.pgonline.co.uk
2022

PG ONLINE

PREFACE

Absolute clarity! That's the aim.

This is everything you need to ace the question on Macbeth and beam with pride. The content is laid out in a beautifully illustrated format that is clear, approachable and as concise and simple as possible.

The checklist on the contents pages will help you keep track of what you have already worked through and what's left before the big day.

We have included worked exam-style questions with answers. There is also an exam-style question at the end of the book. You can check your answers against those given on page 60.

LEVELS OF LEARNING

Based on the degree to which you are able to truly understand a new topic, we recommend that you work in stages. Start by reading a short explanation of something, then try and recall what you've just read. This will have limited effect if you stop there but it aids the next stage. Question everything. Write down your own summary and then complete and mark a related exam-style question. Cover up the answers if necessary but learn from them once you've seen them. Lastly, teach someone else. Explain the topic in a way that they can understand. Have a go at the different practice questions – they offer an insight into how and where marks are awarded.

Design and artwork: Jessica Webb / PG Online Ltd

First edition 2022   10 9 8 7 6 5 4 3 2 1
A catalogue entry for this book is available from the British Library
ISBN: 978-1-910523-46-9
Copyright © PG Online 2022
All rights reserved
No part of this publication may be reproduced, stored in a retrieval system, or transmitted in any form or by any means without the prior written permission of the copyright owner.

Printed on FSC certified paper by Bell and Bain Ltd, Glasgow, UK.

THE SCIENCE OF REVISION

Illustrations and words

Research has shown that revising with words and pictures doubles the quality of responses by students.[1] This is known as 'dual-coding' because it provides two ways of fetching the information from our brain. The improvement in responses is particularly apparent in students when they are asked to apply their knowledge to different problems. Recall, application and judgement are all specifically and carefully assessed in public examination questions.

Retrieval of information

Retrieval practice encourages students to come up with answers to questions.[2] The closer the question is to one you might see in a real examination, the better. Also, the closer the environment in which a student revises is to the 'examination environment', the better. Students who had a test 2–7 days away did 30% better using retrieval practice than students who simply read, or repeatedly reread material. Students who were expected to teach the content to someone else after their revision period did better still.[3] What was found to be most interesting in other studies is that students using retrieval methods and testing for revision were also more resilient to the introduction of stress.[4]

Ebbinghaus' forgetting curve and spaced learning

Ebbinghaus' 140-year-old study examined the rate at which we forget things over time. The findings still hold true. However, the act of forgetting facts and techniques and relearning them is what cements them into the brain.[5] Spacing out revision is more effective than cramming – we know that, but students should also know that the space between revisiting material should vary depending on how far away the examination is. A cyclical approach is required. An examination 12 months away necessitates revisiting covered material about once a month. A test in 30 days should have topics revisited every 3 days – intervals of roughly a tenth of the time available.[6]

Summary

Students: the more tests and past questions you do, in an environment as close to examination conditions as possible, the better you are likely to perform on the day. If you prefer to listen to music while you revise, tunes without lyrics will be far less detrimental to your memory and retention. Silence is most effective.[5] If you choose to study with friends, choose carefully – effort is contagious.[7]

---

1. Mayer, R. E., & Anderson, R. B. (1991). Animations need narrations: An experimental test of dual-coding hypothesis. *Journal of Education Psychology*, (83)4, 484–490.
2. Roediger III, H. L., & Karpicke, J.D. (2006). Test-enhanced learning: Taking memory tests improves long-term retention. *Psychological Science*, 17(3), 249–255.
3. Nestojko, J., Bui, D., Kornell, N. & Bjork, E. (2014). Expecting to teach enhances learning and organisation of knowledge in free recall of text passages. *Memory and Cognition*, 42(7), 1038–1048.
4. Smith, A. M., Floerke, V. A., & Thomas, A. K. (2016) Retrieval practice protects memory against acute stress. *Science*, 354(6315), 1046–1048.
5. Perham, N., & Currie, H. (2014). Does listening to preferred music improve comprehension performance? *Applied Cognitive Psychology*, 28(2), 279–284.
6. Cepeda, N. J., Vul, E., Rohrer, D., Wixted, J. T. & Pashler, H. (2008). Spacing effects in learning a temporal ridgeline of optimal retention. *Psychological Science*, 19(11), 1095–1102.
7. Busch, B. & Watson, E. (2019), *The Science of Learning*, 1st ed. Routledge.

CONTENTS

Assessment objectives vi

Context, language and structure

Shakespeare and *Macbeth* 2
Context 3
Features of plays 6
Shakespeare's language 7
Language techniques 10

Analysis of acts

Act 1, Scenes 1–2 12
Act 1, Scene 3 13
Act 1, Scene 4 15
Act 1, Scenes 5–6 16
Act 1, Scene 7 17
Act 2, Scenes 1–2 18
Act 2, Scene 3 20
Act 2, Scenes 3–4 21
Act 3, Scene 1 22
Act 3, Scene 2–3 23
Act 3, Scene 4 24
Act 3, Scene 5–6 25
Act 4, Scene 1 26
Act 4, Scene 1–2 27
Act 4, Scene 3 28
Act 5, Scene 1 29
Act 5, Scene 2–4 30
Act 5, Scene 5–6 31
Act 5, Scene 7–8 32

Analysis of characters

Characters: Macbeth 33
Characters: Lady Macbeth 38
Characters: Banquo 42
Characters: Duncan 43
Characters: The Witches 44
Characters: Macduff 45
Characters: Malcolm and Donalbain 46

Analysis of themes

Themes: Ambition 47
Themes: Supernatural 50
Themes: Appearance and reality 54
Themes: Kingship 56

Examination practice 59
Examination practice answers 60
Levels-based mark schemes for extended response questions 61
Index 62
Acknowledgements 64
Examination tips 65

MARK ALLOCATIONS

All the questions in this book require extended responses. These answers should be marked as a whole in accordance with the levels of response guidance on **page 61**. The answers provided are examples only. There are many more points to make than there are marks available, so the answers are not exhaustive.

ASSESSMENT OBJECTIVES

In the exam, your answers will be marked against assessment objectives (AOs). It's important you understand which skills each AO tests.

AO1
- Show the ability to read, understand and respond to texts.
- Answers should maintain a critical style and develop an informed personal response.
- Use examples from the text, including quotes, to support and illustrate points.

AO2
- Analyse the language, form and structure used by a writer to create meanings and effects, using relevant subject terminology where appropriate.

AO3
- Show understanding of the relationships between texts and the contexts in which they were written.

AO4
- Use a range of vocabulary and sentence structures for clarity, purpose and effect, with accurate spelling and punctuation.

The AOs on this page have been written in simple language. See the AQA website for the official wording.

PAPER 1
Shakespeare and the 19th-century novel

Information about Paper 1

Written exam: 1 hour 45 minutes (this includes the question on the 19th-century novel)

64 marks (30 marks for Shakespeare plus 4 marks for SPaG, and 30 marks for 19th-century novel)

40% of the qualification grade (20% each for Shakespeare and the 19th-century novel)

Questions
One extended-writing question per text

SHAKESPEARE AND *MACBETH*

Macbeth is a play by William Shakespeare. It's not known exactly when it was written, but it was thought to have been first performed in 1606.

William Shakespeare

William Shakespeare (1564–1616) is one of the best-known English authors. He's most famous for his plays (he wrote at least 37 in his lifetime), but he also wrote poetry. His plays can be broadly grouped into: **comedies** (humorous plays), **histories** (plays about historical figures) and **tragedies** (plays with an unhappy ending). *Macbeth* is one of his most famous tragedies.

> The full title of the play is *The Tragedie of Macbeth*.

William Shakespeare

Tragedies

Tragedies have been written since the time of Ancient Greece, and they usually have the following features:

1

A **protagonist** (main character) who is of high social standing (e.g. a king or noble).	Macbeth is the Thane of Glamis (Lord of Glamis), a Scottish noble.

2

The protagonist has a **fatal flaw** (a characteristic which contributes to their downfall).	Macbeth's ambition and desire for power results in his undoing.

3

An **antagonist** (the protagonist's rival) who helps bring about the demise of the protagonist.	Macduff acts as the play's antagonist, eventually killing Macbeth.

> Tragedies are supposed to provoke **catharsis** from the audience. Catharsis describes a purging of emotions through art.

CONTEXT

Macbeth was written for a 17th-century audience. The context of the 1600s is important for understanding the deeper meaning of the play.

History

Macbeth is set in Scotland during the 11th century. Although the play is very loosely based on real people, most of the play's events are fictional.

> ⭐ You need to comment on the play's context to get marks for AO3 (see **page vi**).

King James I

James (right) was King James VI of Scotland, and after Queen Elizabeth I died in 1603, he also became King James I of England and Ireland. James claimed to be descended from Banquo, so the procession of kings that Macbeth sees in Act 4, Scene 1 is a reference to James' lineage.

King James I (1566–1625)

In Act 4, Scene 1, Macbeth sees some of Banquo's descendants carrying *"treble sceptres"*. This is a reference to James being ruler of three countries: England, Scotland and Ireland.

Comment: James I sponsored Shakespeare's acting company, and it became known as The King's Men, so Shakespeare would have been careful to present Banquo in a flattering way.

Divine Right of Kings

During the Middle Ages and the medieval period, people believed in the **Divine Right of Kings**. This meant that the king (or queen) was appointed by God, and overthrowing a monarch was comparable to directly disobeying God. Since most people in the 17th century were religious, the idea of overthrowing the king would have been abhorrent.

Macbeth renounces the Divine Right when he murders Duncan. As a result, terrible things happen to Macbeth and to Scotland. The play is a warning to anyone contemplating **regicide** (killing a monarch). (See the Gunpowder Plot on **page 4**.)

Religion

Religion was very important in 17th-century Britain and most people would have followed a version of Christianity. Witchcraft (see **page 4**) was seen as the work of the devil.

Witchcraft

King James was obsessed with witchcraft. He wrote a book called *Daemonologie*, which describes different types of demons and how they torment humans. It's thought that this book influenced *Macbeth*. King James believed witches were specifically targeting him. For example, he thought witches had sent storms to try to shipwreck him when he travelled across the North Sea.

A woodcut showing two witches and a demonic beast

Comment: The Witches curse a sailor with stormy seas in Act 1, Scene 3. This could be a reference to the storm supposedly sent to kill King James.

Witches were often blamed for people's misfortune, for example illness, failed crops or bad weather. King James made witchcraft a capital offence, meaning that anyone accused of being a witch could be executed. This led to witch hunts, where thousands of people (usually women) were sentenced to death. There was a lot of hysteria around witchcraft at the time *Macbeth* was written, so audiences would have been frightened, but also fascinated, by witches.

Comment: The supernatural elements in *Macbeth* would have provided a spectacle for the audience. Shakespeare may have used gunpowder to create flashes and bangs to simulate lightning, and sulphur (a chemical in gunpowder) has a smell like rotten eggs, which could have created the "*filthy air*" described by the Witches in Act 1, Scene 1.

Gunpowder Plot, 1605

A year before *Macbeth* was performed, Guy Fawkes and his accomplices attempted to blow up the Houses of Parliament and kill King James. The plot was uncovered before the explosion, and the plotters were executed. The idea of regicide is central to *Macbeth*.

Comment: One of the plotters executed for his involvement in the Gunpowder Plot was accused of equivocation (using ambiguous language to conceal the truth). The porter in Act 2, Scene 3 pokes fun at an "*equivocator*". This is a direct reference to the plotter, and would have been **satirical** humour to 17th-century audiences.

Warfare

During the 16th century, England was involved in numerous wars abroad. Audiences would have been accustomed to the idea of battles and warfare.

Comment: The play opens and closes with a battle which gives *Macbeth* a **cyclical structure** (texts with this structure start and end with similar ideas or events). Structuring the play in this way could be an indication that everything has returned to normal in Scotland by the end of the play.

Satire is the use of humour to mock people, particularly those in politics or involved in current affairs.

Gender roles

In the 17th century, gender roles were fixed. Society was **patriarchal**, where a man was the head of the household, and a woman was supposed to be subservient to her husband and father.

> **Comment:** Lady Macbeth's domineering character and her control over Macbeth would have gone against typical gender roles in the 17th century. She goads Macbeth by questioning his masculinity and she rejects her own femininity when she calls on spirits to "*unsex*" her. These unconventional attitudes towards gender would have shocked Shakespearian audiences.
>
> Some of the most honourable characters, such as Macduff and Malcolm, embrace emotions that are more typically associated with women. They want to "*Weep our sad bosoms empty*" at the sorry state of Scotland. Shakespeare could be suggesting that being a 'good man' does not always equate to having solely 'male' traits.

At the beginning of the play, Lady Macbeth controls and manipulates her husband.

The theatre

In the 16th and 17th centuries, going to the theatre was very popular with both rich and poor people, so there was a lot of demand for new plays. Richer audience members would have sat in covered balconies, whereas poorer audience members would have stood in front of the stage in an area known as the pit, which was open to the elements.

It was illegal for women to perform onstage, so female roles were played by male actors, usually young boys. This means that Lady Macbeth, the Witches and Lady Macduff would have all been played by men and boys originally.

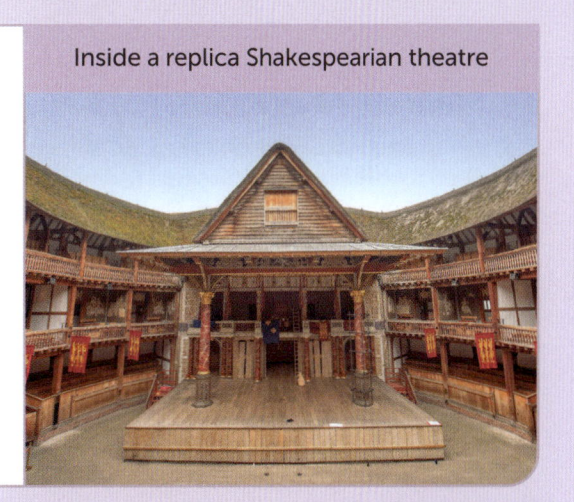

Inside a replica Shakespearian theatre

GCSE English Literature | Macbeth

FEATURES OF PLAYS

Plays are written to be performed, rather than read, so there are features in playscripts that are different to novels.

Acts and scenes

There are five **acts** in *Macbeth*, and each act is broken down into **scenes**. A new scene starts when the setting changes location.

The lines in *Macbeth* are usually numbered. Numbering tends to restart with each new scene. Line numbers help readers navigate the script more easily.

Stage directions

Stage directions are used to tell a director how the play should be performed and to guide the actors. Some stage directions tell actors when to enter or exit the stage or how to deliver a line, whereas other stage directions help to create a certain atmosphere or create tension, for example, information about settings or sound effects.

Enter LADY MACBETH, reading a letter

Stage directions aren't supposed to be spoken.

Exeunt — This means that more than one actor should leave the stage.

Aside — This means that the actor should say or do something away from the other characters.

When a character says their lines aside, this can be used to reveal a character's true feelings about something or to show that a character is behaving in a secretive way. It can also help to create **dramatic irony** (see **page 11**).

'Shakespeare's Globe', a reconstruction of the Globe Theatre

Thunder. Enter the three Witches.

Drum within. — *within* means that the sound is happening off stage.

A cavern. In the middle, a boiling cauldron. Thunder.

Most of Shakespeare's stage directions are brief. This is probably because Shakespeare would have directed his own plays, so knew exactly how he wanted them to be staged.

17th-century productions of *Macbeth* would have created the sound of thunder by rolling a cannon ball along the floor.

SHAKESPEARE'S LANGUAGE

Shakespeare's plays were written over 400 years ago, so the language and punctuation can be tricky for modern-day audiences to understand.

Pronouns

In the 17th century, people used second-person pronouns that are no longer used today:

thou / thee – you

thy – your

thine – yours

The pronoun 'you' is sometimes spelt 'ye'.

Apostrophes

Sometimes letters have been removed from words and replaced with apostrophes. This can be done to adjust the number of syllables in the line and maintain the rhythm of the text.

That look not like the inhabitants o' the earth,

And yet ye are on't?

---

*That look not like the inhabitants **of** the earth,*

*And yet ye are **on it**?*

For more information about the text's rhythm, turn to **pages 8–9**.

Verbs

Some verbs are written with '-(s)t' at the end, for example 'didst', 'hadst', 'art'. These verbs agreed with the second person pronouns 'thou' and 'thee'. If you remove the 'st', the verb should be recognisable.

Thou didst	You did
Thee hadst	You had
Thou art	You are

Some verbs are written with '-th' at the end. For example, 'hath' and 'doth'. These verbs agree with third person pronouns, e.g. 'he', 'she' and 'it'. If you remove the '-th', you should be able to recognise the verb.

He hath	He has
It doth	It does

GCSE **English Literature** | Macbeth

Sentence order

The order that words appear in a sentence can sometimes seem unfamiliar. This is partly because word order was less fixed during Shakespeare's time, so words could be reordered to suit the rhythm of the lines.

Know you not he has? – Don't you know that he has?

Rhythm and speech patterns

Verse

Most of the characters in *Macbeth* speak in **blank verse**. This means their lines don't rhyme, but they have a set rhythm, usually iambic pentameter.

Iambic pentameter

The majority of *Macbeth* is written in **iambic pentameter**. This is a specific rhythm where each line has ten syllables which alternate between unstressed and stressed syllables.

*So **foul** and **fair** a **day** I **have** not **seen**.*

Shared lines

Occasionally, characters might split a line of iambic verse. This can show a close relationship between characters.
For example, in Act 2, Scene 2, Lady Macbeth and Macbeth share lines as they conspire after Duncan's murder.

Lady Macbeth	*Did **not** you **speak**?*
Macbeth	*When?*
Lady Macbeth	*Now.*
Macbeth	*As I descended?*

The Macbeths' dialogue in Act 2, Scene 2 shows their closeness.

Rhythm and speech patterns continued

Trochaic tetrameter

There are a few instances of **trochaic tetrameter** in *Macbeth*. This rhythm has eight syllables in each line, rather than the ten used in iambic pentameter. The patterns of stress are also reversed, so that a stressed syllable follows an unstressed syllable.

The Witches use trochaic tetrameter. This makes their lines contrast with the rhythm of other characters, making their speech sound unusual and unnatural.

> *Dou*ble, *dou*ble **toil** and **trou**ble

Rhyming couplets

Rhyming couplets are two lines written in iambic pentameter which rhyme. They are sometimes used for emphasis at the end of a **soliloquy** (see **page 10**) or the closing lines of a scene, for example, the Doctor's lines at the end of Act 5, Scene 1.

> *Were I from Dunsinane away and clear,*
> *Profit again should hardly draw me here.*

The Witches often speak using rhyming couplets. This makes their speech sound melodious, as if they are chanting or casting a spell.

> *When shall we three meet again*
> *In thunder, lightning or in rain?*

Comment: The Witches sometimes speak in unison. This makes their speech seem eerie and unnatural.

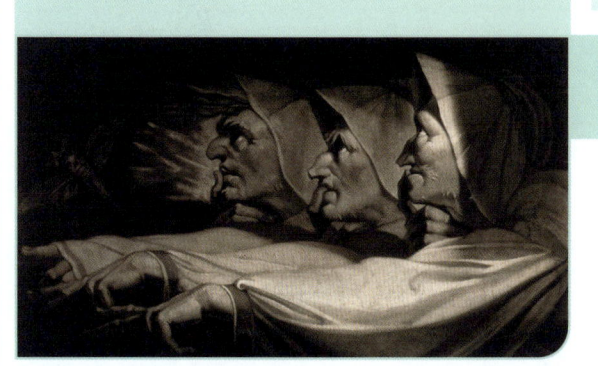

Prose

Prose describes speech without a set rhythm. It is used to show that a character is of a lower class, for example the porter in Act 2, Scene 3.

> *Knock, knock, knock! Who's there? Faith, here's an English tailor come hither for stealing out of a French hose. Come in, tailor. Here you may roast your goose.*

Lady Macbeth's lines in Act 5, Scene 1 are written in prose when she is sleepwalking. Elsewhere, she speaks using iambic pentameter, so this change of rhythm shows her disturbed state of mind.

> *The thane of Fife had a wife. Where is she now?—What, will these hands ne'er be clean?—No more o' that, my lord, no more o' that. You mar all with this starting.*

A print of the Witches

LANGUAGE TECHNIQUES

Shakespeare uses a lot of linguistic and dramatic techniques in *Macbeth*.

Symbolism

Symbolism is when objects, colours or characters represent concepts. There are plenty of examples of symbolism in *Macbeth*. Here are a few of the most recognisable ones.

Bloody hands

Blood in *Macbeth* symbolises guilt. One example of this is in Act 2, Scene 2, when Macbeth questions: "*Will all great Neptune's ocean wash this blood / Clean from my hand?*" Macbeth is implying that he feels so guilty over Duncan's murder that his hands will never be truly clean again. This **foreshadows** (see **page 11**) Lady Macbeth's guilt in Act 5, Scene 1: "*will these hands ne'er be clean?*"

Sleep

Just like bloody hands, sleeplessness symbolises guilt. In Act 2, Scene 2, Macbeth thinks he hears a voice say "*Macbeth doth murder sleep.*" In Act 3, Scene 2, Macbeth admits he's been having nightmares ("*these terrible dreams / That shake us nightly*") and that he's envious of Duncan in death because "*After life's fitful fever he sleeps well*". The references to sleeplessness foreshadow Lady Macbeth's sleepwalking in Act 5, Scene 1.

Weather

Stormy weather in *Macbeth* reflects the chaos and turmoil that Macbeth's actions have brought. For example, the night that Duncan is murdered there is an "*unruly*" storm, and Lennox hears "*strange screams of death.*" The stormy weather links back to the Witches who enter the stage in Act 1, Scene 1 to "***Thunder and lightning***".

> Shakespeare also uses imagery of planting and growing to symbolise being nurtured by a good king. See **page 57** for more.

Soliloquies

A **soliloquy** is a dramatic technique. It describes a moment in a play where a character speaks their thoughts aloud. Soliloquies are usually directed at the audience, rather than other characters, allowing the audience to understand that character's innermost feelings. For example, Macbeth's soliloquy in Act 1, Scene 3 reveals his thoughts about murdering Duncan.

Dramatic irony

This is when the audience knows more than the characters. For example, the audience knows in Act 1, Scene 2 that Duncan intends to make Macbeth Thane of Cawdor, so when the Witches make this prediction to Macbeth in the following scene, the audience already knows their prediction will come true.

Foreshadowing

Foreshadowing hints at something that will happen later in the play. It can be used to create tension or a sense of unease amongst the audience. For example, Macbeth's bloodied hands in Act 2, Scene 2 foreshadow the imaginary blood on Lady Macbeth's hands in Act 5, Scene 1.

Antithesis

Shakespeare frequently uses examples of **antithesis** in *Macbeth*. This is when two opposing ideas are joined together in a line, for example "*Fair is foul*". This linguistic technique is used to represent the idea of deception, and that not everything is as it seems. For more on the theme of appearance and reality, turn to **page 54**.

Imagery

Shakespeare uses **imagery** to convey meaning to the audience in a creative way. For example, when Donalbain discovers his father has been murdered, he uses the metaphor: "*There's daggers in men's smiles.*" This line highlights the theme of deception, suggesting that someone who appears friendly, may be disguising murderous thoughts. The imagery of dagger-sharp teeth is also frightening, and links to the dagger used to murder Duncan.

Foil

A **foil** describes a character who is the opposite to another character. Writers use foils to reveal information about one character by contrasting their behaviour and emotions with another. Banquo is a foil to Macbeth, because although the Witches predict his descendants will become kings, his honour prevents him from doing anything criminal to make the prediction come true, which is the opposite to how Macbeth behaves.

Puns

Puns describe when words with a double meaning are used deliberately. Puns are more often found in Shakespeare's comedies, but there are some examples in *Macbeth*. For example, in Act 3, Scene 1, Macbeth describes Banquo's advice as "*grave*", which can mean 'serious' but since Macbeth is planning to murder Banquo, it also has the meaning of 'a place where a corpse is laid to rest'.

ACT 1

Act 1 introduces most of the major characters and establishes the key themes of the play.

Act 1, Scene 1

The play opens with *"Thunder and lightning"*.

Comment: Thunder and lightning creates an ominous mood, and connects the Witches to the stormy weather in Act 2, Scene 3.

Three Witches decide when and where they will meet Macbeth.

Comment: The Witches speak in **rhyming couplets**, which makes their speech sound unnatural, as if they are invoking a spell. This hints at their **supernatural** nature. For more on rhythm and speech patterns in *Macbeth*, turn to **pages 8–9**.

The scene closes with the line, *"Fair is foul, and foul is fair"*. The Witches often use **antithesis** (see **page 11**) in their speech, and this contradictory language reinforces the theme of **appearance and reality** (see **page 54**). This line suggests something which looks innocent might be *"foul"* which **foreshadows** Macbeth and Lady Macbeth's betrayal of Duncan.

Act 1, Scene 2

The Scottish King, Duncan, and his sons, Malcolm and Donalbain, along with Lennox (a Scottish noble) await news of a battle. The Scottish army are fighting invading Norwegian forces as well as two Scottish rebels, the Thane of Cawdor and Macdonald.

Comment: The battle is a dramatic opening and establishes an atmosphere of violence and conflict. It also foreshadows the battle in Act 5.

A bloodied captain tells the men that Macbeth and Banquo fought bravely and were ferocious in battle: *"Except they meant to bathe in reeking wounds"*.

Comment: This is the audience's first introduction to Macbeth's character. In the context of battle, Macbeth's violence is worthy of praise. He is presented as a fearless, savage soldier, but the image of him bathing in blood foreshadows the bloodshed yet to come. See **pages 33–35** for more on the character of Macbeth.

A bloodied captain tells Duncan about the battle

Act 1, Scene 2 continued

Ross (another Scottish noble) enters, and describes how Macbeth captured the traitorous Thane of Cawdor and that the Norwegian king is now pleading for a peace treaty. Duncan decides to give Macbeth the title of Thane of Cawdor as a reward for his loyalty and victory.

Comment: Duncan is presented as a generous king. For more on the character of Duncan, see **page 43**.

Act 1, Scene 3

The Witches enter. One of the Witches intends to curse a sailor with sleeplessness after his wife refused to give her any chestnuts: *"I'll drain him dry as hay. / Sleep shall neither night nor day"*. The other two Witches help her create a storm to stop the sailor from sleeping for 81 weeks.

The storm the Witches create is reminiscent of the storm that King James believed was sent by witches to kill him. (See **page 3**.)

Comment: This presents the witches as powerful, supernatural beings who are petty, malicious and vindictive, leading the audience to believe that Macbeth may be their next victim. For more on the character of the Witches, see **page 44**.

Banquo and Macbeth enter.

Comment: Macbeth's first line, *"So foul and fair a day I have not seen"*, repeats the Witches use of antithesis in the line *"Fair is foul"*. This hints that Macbeth has a connection with the Witches.

The Witches speak to Macbeth and Banquo and predict that Macbeth will be given the title of Thane of Cawdor.

Comment: This is an example of **dramatic irony**. The audience already knows from Act 1, Scene 2 that Duncan intends to give Macbeth this title.

They also predict that Macbeth will become King of Scotland. Immediately, Macbeth seems afraid of the prediction. Banquo comments: *"why do you start and seem to fear / Things that so sound so fair?"*.

Comment: Macbeth's reaction suggests he is filled with dread at the news, implying that he already knows he will have to do a terrible thing to make the prophecy come true.

The Witches tell Banquo that his descendants will be kings one day using ambiguous language: *"Lesser than Macbeth and greater / Not so happy, yet much happier"*.

Comment: This is another example of the Witches using **antithesis**. Speaking in riddles emphasises their duplicitous nature, suggesting that they aren't telling the whole truth, and are deliberately trying to mislead Macbeth and Banquo.

Act 1, Scene 3 continued

The Witches vanish: "*Melted, as breath into the wind*".

Comment: The Witches' sudden and mysterious exit shows their supernatural ability. It's likely that the Witches would have exited via a trapdoor in the stage floor. This would have signalled to the audience that the Witches have returned to hell.

Ross and Angus enter, and tell Macbeth that he has been given the title Thane of Cawdor. This proves to Macbeth that the Witches' prophecies are genuine.

Comment: Banquo is mistrustful of the Witches: "*And oftentimes, to win us our harm, / The instruments of darkness tell us truths*". He suspects that the Witches are deliberately manipulating them to cause chaos. This suggests that Banquo is perceptive and cannot be easily deceived. For more on Banquo's character, turn to **page 42**.

Although Macbeth is also wary of the Witches ("*Cannot be ill, cannot be good*"), his ambition makes him want to ignore the possibility that the Witches are trying to deceive him. Macbeth's ambition makes him easy to manipulate, see **page 47.**

Almost straight away, Macbeth thinks about killing Duncan to make the prophecy come true. "*My thought, whose murder yet is but fantastical, / Shakes so my single state of man*".

Comment: Macbeth's murderous thoughts shows how ambitious he is. He's prepared to kill to achieve power. However, his soliloquy shows he's conflicted about committing murder in Act 1. This contrasts with the murders of Banquo in Act 2 and the Macduffs in Act 3 where Macbeth arranges the killings without hesitation.

Macbeth also realises that if he's destined to become king, then he may not need to do anything to make the prophecy come true: "*If chance will have me king, why chance may crown me / Without my stir*".

Comment: Macbeth reasons that if he's destined to become king, then he doesn't need to do anything to make it happen. However, later in the play, Macbeth murders Banquo to try to change the course of fate and stop Banquo's descendants from becoming king.

Act 1, Scene 4

Duncan, Lennox, Malcolm and Donalbain discuss the execution of the traitorous Thane of Cawdor. Duncan reflects that he trusted the Thane of Cawdor, and he never would have suspected that he would betray him: "*There's no art / To find the mind's construction in the face. / He was a gentleman on whom I built / An absolute trust.*"

Comment: This demonstrates Duncan's trusting nature, and suggests that Duncan will be easily betrayed again. Immediately after Duncan says these lines, Macbeth enters the stage, making the **dramatic irony** of these lines clear to the audience.

Macbeth, Banquo, Ross and Angus enter. Duncan praises Macbeth for his bravery in battle: "*The sin of my ingratitude even now / Was heavy on me.*"

Comment: Duncan is a grateful and appreciative king. Presenting Duncan as a good man makes his murder even more shocking. For more on the character of Duncan, see **page 43**.

Duncan tells the men that Malcolm has been made Prince of Cumberland, and will be next in line to the Scottish throne. To himself, Macbeth says: "*The Prince of Cumberland! That is a step / On which I must fall down, or else o'erleap.*"

Comment: Macbeth recognises that Malcolm might be an obstacle to him becoming king. Macbeth's ambition makes him think of murder again: "*Stars hide your fires; / Let not light see my black and deep desires.*" Macbeth uses verse in these lines, which echoes the speech of the Witches, and makes Macbeth sound as though he's reciting a spell. This further connects him to the Witches, and the theme of the supernatural.

The characters decide to travel to Inverness to stay at Macbeth's castle.

Act 1, Scene 5

Lady Macbeth reads a letter from her husband which tells her about his meeting with the Witches and the prophecies they made.

Lady Macbeth immediately assumes that they will kill Duncan to make the prophecy come true, but she worries that her husband is too gentle to go through with the murder: "*Yet I do fear thy nature; / It is too full o' th' milk of human kindness.*"

> **Comment:** Lady Macbeth's assumption that they will kill Duncan suggests she is just as ambitious and power-hungry as Macbeth. She doesn't need convincing to commit murder. For more on Lady Macbeth's ambition, turn to **page 47**.

A servant enters and informs Lady Macbeth that her husband and King Duncan are on their way to the castle. Lady Macbeth performs a **soliloquy** telling the audience of her intention to kill Duncan that evening. She calls on the spirits, requesting that they "*fill me from the crown to the toe top-full / Of direst cruelty.*"

> **Comment:** Lady Macbeth's reference to spirits reinforces the theme of the supernatural.

Macbeth enters, and they discuss killing Duncan that night. Lady Macbeth encourages Macbeth to be deceitful: "*Look like th' innocent flower, / But be the serpent 't.*"

> **Comment:** Just like the previous Thane of Cawdor, the Macbeths' plan to deceive King Duncan and betray him. For more on the theme of appearance and reality, turn to **page 54**.

Act 1, Scene 6

Duncan, Banquo, Malcolm, Donalbain, Lennox, Macduff, Ross and Angus arrive at Macbeth's castle in Inverness. Duncan comments on how pleasant the air is: "*the air / Nimbly and sweetly recommends itself.*"

> **Comment:** This adds to the **dramatic irony**. Duncan is delighted to be at Macbeth's castle, but he is unaware that he is walking into a trap.

Lady Macbeth welcomes her visitors, disguising her true intentions. Duncan remarks that Macbeth has not come with Lady Macbeth to greet his guests.

> **Comment:** Macbeth's absence suggests that he cannot bear to welcome Duncan when he plans to kill him. This suggests that deception does not come as easily to Macbeth as it does to Lady Macbeth.

Act 1, Scene 7

Macbeth opens this scene with a soliloquy, debating whether he should commit the murder. He comments that bad deeds often come back to haunt people: *"this even-handed justice / Commends the ingredients of our poison'd chalice / To our own lips."*

Comment: This is ironic. Macbeth knows that his actions will come back to haunt him, but he eventually decides to commit the murder anyway. His ambition has made him blind to sense.

Macbeth remarks that his betrayal would be even worse because Duncan is a guest in his home and because he is a good king: *"hath been / So clear in his great office."*

Comment: The play frequently references kingship, and the qualities needed to be a good monarch. For more on the theme of kingship, turn to **page 56**.

Lady Macbeth enters, and Macbeth initially refuses to murder Duncan: *"We will proceed no further in this business."*

Comment: Macbeth's indecisiveness suggests that he's not truly evil at this point in the play. He still has a conscience.

Lady Macbeth is furious at her husband's change of heart. She goads him and calls him a *"coward"*, telling him that she would have beaten her own infant if she had promised Macbeth she would.

Comment: Lady Macbeth's comment about murdering her own child is shocking. At this point in the play, she is presented as the crueller, more aggressive character. She bullies her husband and questions his bravery in order to manipulate him. Lady Macbeth's behaviour would have been shocking to 17th-century audiences, who would expect women to be gentle and subservient. For more on the character of Lady Macbeth, turn to **page 38**.

Lady Macbeth plans to sneak into Duncan's bedroom as he sleeps. She proposes they get Duncan's servants drunk so they sleep through everything, and then blame them for the murder. Macbeth is eventually convinced. He praises her, saying that she should only give birth to sons because she is so fearless: *"Bring forth men-children only, / For thy undaunted mettle should compose / Nothing but males."* He agrees to kill Duncan, and tells Lady Macbeth to deceive her guests: *"False face must hide what false heart doth know."*

Comment: Act 1 ends with a key moment: the Macbeths agree to murder Duncan. This influences the characters' actions for the remainder of the play.

ACT 2

Act 2 deals with Duncan's murder and the repercussions of his death.

Act 2, Scene 1

Banquo and his son, Fleance, enter. Banquo admits to Fleance that he doesn't want to fall asleep because evil thoughts come to him at night: "*Merciful powers, / Restrain in me the cursèd thoughts that nature / Gives way to in repose.*"

Comment: This implies that Banquo has also been struggling to deny his ambitions. The Witches' prophecy that his descendants will be kings is tempting him to do evil things.

Macbeth enters and Banquo is surprised that he is not asleep. Banquo admits that he has dreamed about the Witches and their prophecies. Macbeth lies and tells Banquo: "*I think not of them*" but that he would like to talk to Banquo about the prophecies at some point. Macbeth cryptically tells Banquo that if Banquo is loyal, Macbeth will reward him. Banquo replies "*So I lose none / In seeking to augment it.*" Banquo will only stay loyal to Macbeth if his conscience remains clear.

Comment: Banquo believes in honour above ambition. He is a **foil** to Macbeth (see **page 11**).

Banquo and Fleance exit. Macbeth performs another soliloquy. He sees a ghostly dagger in front of him. It's unclear whether the dagger is real or just a figment of Macbeth's imagination.

Comment: The ghostly dagger is another symbol of the theme of the supernatural. See **page 51** for more.

Act 2, Scene 2

Lady Macbeth waits for Macbeth to kill Duncan. She is afraid that the servants woke up and the plan is ruined. She comments that she would have killed Duncan herself if he hadn't looked so much like her own father.

Comment: Lady Macbeth's comment that Duncan reminded her of her father is her first show of sensitivity.

Macbeth returns from killing Duncan.

Comment: Unlike other murders later in the play, Duncan's murder happens off-stage. This is probably because it was a terrible crime to commit regicide (see **page 3**).

Macbeth returns to Lady Macbeth with bloodied hands and daggers

Act 2, Scene 2 continued

Macbeth comments how he was unable to say the word *"Amen"*.

Comment: Being unable to say *"Amen"* suggests Macbeth has become ungodly and evil. Macbeth has gone against God's will by disrupting the Divine Right of Kings (see **page 3**).

The murder has affected Macbeth. He's paranoid and imagines that he heard voices crying out *"Sleep no more! / Macbeth does murder sleep!"*

Comment: Macbeth's reaction to the murder is the first hint of madness and guilt to come. It also foreshadows Lady Macbeth's sleepwalking in Act 5, Scene 1.

In his panic, Macbeth has forgotten to smear blood on the sleeping servants and plant the daggers next to them. Macbeth refuses to go back to the scene, *"I am afraid to think what I have done."* Instead, Lady Macbeth returns to the scene of the murder to frame the servants. While Lady Macbeth is off-stage, Macbeth hears a knocking sound, and is overcome with guilt *"Will all great Neptune's ocean wash this blood / Clean from my hand?"*

Comment: The reference to washing bloody hands foreshadows Lady Macbeth's compulsive handwashing when she sleepwalks in Act 5, Scene 1.

Lady Macbeth re-enters and is furious at Macbeth's cowardice. She remarks: *"My hands are of your colour, but I shame / To wear a heart so white."* The Macbeths prepare to return to their bedroom to wash their hands: *"A little water clears us of this deed."*

Comment: Lady Macbeth wrongly thinks that washing their hands will rid them of guilt. It's another reference to her handwashing in Act 5, Scene 1.

The Macbeths hear more knocking off-stage.

Comment: The knocking sound reminds the audience of a comment Macbeth made in Act 1, Scene 3: *"And make my seated heart knock at my ribs"*. The knocking could symbolise Macbeth's racing heart and his guilt.

Macbeth ends the scene by commenting: *"Wake Duncan with thy knocking. I wish thou couldst."*

Comment: This shows Macbeth's remorse. Although he's committed a terrible crime, he still has a conscience at this point. This contrasts with his lack of remorse after the other murders later in the play.

Act 2, Scene 3

A porter enters to the sound of knocking.

Comment: The continuation of the knocking sound shows that this scene is happening at the same time as the previous scene.

The porter pretends that he is the gatekeeper of hell, "*Knock, knock knock! Who's there, I' th' name of / Beelzebub?*" (Beelzebub was a name given to the devil).

Comment: The porter pretending to be the gatekeeper of hell is ironic. It draws parallels between Macbeth and the devil.

The porter opens the door to find Macduff and Lennox knocking to be let in.

Comment: The knocking sound that startled the Macbeths in the previous act turns out to be Macduff. This foreshadows Macbeth's fear of Macduff in Acts 4 and 5.

The porter jokes with Macduff and Lennox about drinking too much alcohol.

Comment: The porter's humorous speech about the effects of alcohol decrease the tension of the previous scene, and provide some **comic relief** to the audience.

Macbeth enters, and Macduff asks if the king is awake yet. Macduff leaves the stage to go to wake Duncan. Lennox comments on how stormy the previous night was, and that he heard "*screams of death*" and voices "*prophesying with accents terrible / Of dire combustion and confused events.*"

Comment: The audience links Lennox's comments about "*prophesying with accents terrible*" to the Witches. In Act 1, Scene 3, the Witches talk of conjuring a storm, which hints that the Witches were responsible for the stormy weather and will be responsible for the chaos which will follow.

Act 2, Scene 3 continued

Macduff re-enters and announces that the king is dead. Macbeth and Lennox exit to see for themselves. Macduff rings a bell which summons Lady Macbeth. Macduff informs Lady Macbeth that Duncan is dead and says: *"O gentle lady, / 'Tis not for you to hear what I can speak: / The repetition, in a woman's ear, / Would murder as it fell."*

> **Comment:** Macduff refuses to tell Lady Macbeth what has happened as he thinks she's too sensitive and delicate to hear about the murder. The audience recognises the irony of this.

Banquo, Macbeth and Ross enter. Macbeth pretends to be distraught by the news. Malcolm and Donalbain enter, and they too are told that Duncan is dead. Lennox remarks that the servants must have killed Duncan because they were covered in blood and the murder weapon was next to them. Macbeth admits that he killed the servants out of fury and because of his love for Duncan. Lady Macbeth faints.

> **Comment:** Lady Macbeth fainting could be a deliberate distraction to stop Macbeth from saying any more about killing the servants and to prevent anyone from questioning Macbeth further. Lady Macbeth uses preconceptions about women being weak to her advantage, which shows her cunning nature.

Malcolm and Donalbain speak privately. They suspect, as the king's sons, that they are in danger. Malcolm decides to flee to England, and Donalbain decides to flee to Ireland.

Act 2, Scene 4

Ross and an Old Man discuss the previous night's storm and how the sun has failed to rise that morning: *"And yet dark night strangles the travelling lamp"*. The Old Man comments that it is *"unnatural"*, and that Duncan's horses broke out of the stalls and started eating each other.

> **Comment:** Since Macbeth has disturbed God's will by murdering Duncan and subverting the Divine Right of Kings, these unnatural events could be interpreted as God's displeasure.

Macduff enters and tells Ross that Malcolm and Donalbain have fled. They suspect that they paid the servants to kill Duncan. Ross remarks that with Malcolm and Donalbain gone, Macbeth will be crowned king. Ross says he will travel to Scone (a place in Scotland) for Macbeth's coronation, but Macduff decides not to attend and instead return to his castle in Fife.

> **Comment:** Macduff's decision to not attend Macbeth's coronation suggests that he is suspicious of Macbeth. For more on the character of Macduff, turn to **page 45**.

ACT 3

The Witches' prophecies about Macbeth have come true, and he's now King of Scotland.

Act 3, Scene 1

Banquo remarks to himself that all the prophecies the Witches made about Macbeth have come true, but he is suspicious of Macbeth: "*I fear / Thou played'st most foully for 't.*"

> **Comment:** This hints that Banquo is a perceptive character. See **page 42** for more on the character of Banquo.

Macbeth and Lady Macbeth, now king and queen, enter, along with Lennox, Ross and other courtiers. Macbeth flatters Banquo by saying that he is the coronation's "*chief guest*". Macbeth enquires whether Banquo will be going riding that evening, and Banquo confirms he will with his son, Fleance.

The Macbeths are now King and Queen of Scotland.

> **Comment:** Macbeth wants to know Banquo's whereabouts so he can arrange for Banquo's murder that evening. This highlights Macbeth's deceitful nature.

Macbeth dismisses everyone except for a servant. He tells the servant to bring in some men who he wishes to speak with. While the servant is off-stage, Macbeth gives a soliloquy. He confesses that he feels insecure in his position as king, and that he's deeply afraid of Banquo, especially since the Witches predicted that Banquo's descendants would be kings.

> **Comment:** Macbeth is afraid of Banquo because he "*hath a wisdom that doth guide his valour*". This is another example of how Banquo acts as a foil to Macbeth.

The servant re-enters with the two men, who are murderers that Macbeth has hired. Macbeth convinces the murderers that it is Banquo's fault that they are poor.

> **Comment:** Previously, Macbeth took action to make sure the Witches' predictions come true. Now, he is taking action to prevent their prediction about Banquo's descendants becoming king from happening. Macbeth is trying to alter the course of fate.

Macbeth questions the murderers' masculinity to convince them to murder Banquo.

> **Comment:** Taunting the murderers' manliness is a similar tactic that Lady Macbeth used in Act 1, Scene 7 to convince Macbeth to murder Duncan.

Act 3, Scene 2

Lady Macbeth begins to show the first signs of remorse and paranoia for killing Duncan, admitting that she'd rather be the victim of murder than the murderer who must live with their actions. ("*'Tis safer to be that which we destroy / Than by destruction dwell in doubtful joy.*")

Comment: Lady Macbeth speaks in rhyming couplets here. This deliberately brings attention and emphasis to what she is saying.

Macbeth enters and he echoes her regret and paranoia, confirming "*Better be with the dead, / Whom we, to gain our peace, have sent to peace.*" Lady Macbeth tells Macbeth to put on a brave face at dinner that evening. Macbeth admits he's paranoid while Banquo is still alive, and hints that he plans to kill Banquo and his son.

Comment: Macbeth's language is full of dark imagery. He speaks of "*scorpions*", "*bats*", "*beetles*" and "*crows*". This echoes the 'ingredients' the Witches use in their potion in Act 4, Scene 1, e.g. "*bat*", "*snake*", "*toad*", which further connects Macbeth and the Witches.

Lady Macbeth isn't involved in the plot to kill Banquo, and Macbeth tries to protect her from the truth: "*Be innocent of the knowledge*".

Comment: Lady Macbeth was the instigator of Duncan's murder, but now the roles have reversed and Macbeth is the driving force behind the plot to kill Banquo. This shows a change in the dynamic between the two characters.

Act 3, Scene 3

Three murderers wait for Banquo and Fleance. They attack and kill Banquo, but Fleance escapes.

Comment: Macbeth has tried to alter the course of fate by attempting to kill Banquo and Fleance, but Fleance's escape suggests that the Witches' prophecy about Banquo's descendants becoming king can still come true. This suggests it's pointless to tamper with fate, and suggests that Macbeth would have become king without killing Duncan.

Act 3, Scene 4

Macbeth and Lady Macbeth host a banquet with the other lords. One of the murderers enters the dining hall and tells Macbeth that he has killed Banquo, but that Fleance has escaped.

During the meal, the ghost of Banquo enters and sits in Macbeth's seat. Macbeth is the only character who can see the ghost, and he is terrified.

Comment: It's unclear whether the ghost is real or a figment of Macbeth's imagination, caused by guilt. The ghost of Banquo is another supernatural element in the play (see **page 50**).

Lady Macbeth tries to excuse Macbeth's behaviour to the other lords by claiming he has suffered from a condition since childhood. Privately, she scolds Macbeth for behaving strangely and questions his masculinity, remarking that his hallucinations are like a "*woman's story*".

Comment: Lady Macbeth taunts Macbeth about his masculinity to try to control him, just like in Act 1, Scene 7.

The ghost of Banquo re-appears and Macbeth says that the ghost taking the form of Banquo is more terrifying than a bear, rhinoceros or tiger. Lady Macbeth remarks that Macbeth's strange behaviour has ruined dinner and tells everyone to leave. Macbeth tries to talk to the guests about the ghost, but Lady Macbeth tells them to ignore Macbeth and leave.

Comment: Lady Macbeth is frightened that Macbeth will reveal Banquo's murder to the guests.

After the guests leave, Macbeth comments to Lady Macbeth that Macduff was absent from the feast, and remarks that he plans to see the Witches tomorrow to ask them what else the future holds.

Comment: Even though he's got what he wanted, Macbeth still feels insecure and needs reassurance from the Witches.

Macbeth acknowledges that he's come too far to turn back: "*I am in blood / Stepped in so far that, should I wade no more, / Returning were as tedious as go o'er.*"

Act 3, Scene 5

Hecate, the goddess of magic, scolds the Witches for tricking Macbeth with riddles without her knowledge. She claims that she needs time to prepare "*a dismal and a fatal end*" for Macbeth.

Comment: Hecate's speech suggest that Macbeth isn't entirely to blame for his own destruction. Supernatural forces are also trying to bring about his downfall.

Some productions of *Macbeth* cut this scene. They believe that it wasn't written by Shakespeare.

Act 3, Scene 6

Lennox and a Lord discuss recent events. Lennox's speech is sarcastic. He implies that Macbeth is responsible for the murders of both Duncan and Banquo, by hinting at the similarities between the two deaths, for example, how the victims' sons have been blamed for the murder: "*Fleance kill'd, / For Fleance fled.*"

Comment: This scene shows other characters are beginning to suspect that Macbeth is responsible for the murders, and he is beginning to lose the loyalty of his subjects.

The Lord responds by calling Macbeth a "*tyrant*". He knows that Macbeth is responsible. The Lord reveals that Malcolm and Macduff have asked the King of England to raise an army to march on Macbeth's castle. Macbeth is aware of the army coming for him, and is preparing for war: "*And this report / Hath so exasperated the king that he / Prepares for some attempt of war.*"

Comment: This increases the tension. The audience knows that there will be a battle.

The Lord tells Lennox that Macbeth sent a messenger ordering Macduff to return to Scotland, and Macduff refused.

ACT 4

There are only three scenes in Act 4, but they establish the conflict between Macbeth and Macduff.

Act 4, Scene 1

The Witches are in a cave, dancing around a cauldron and making a potion with repulsive ingredients: "*eye of newt*", "*toe of frog*", "*tongue of dog*".

Comment: The ingredients the Witches use, including human liver, lips and finger, show their dark and cruel nature.

The Witches know that Macbeth is approaching, and the Second Witch announces, "*Something wicked this way comes.*"

Comment: The Witches describe Macbeth as "*wicked*". This suggests his transformation into an evil character is now complete.

Macbeth enters and demands that the Witches answer his questions.

Comment: Macbeth tries to control the Witches: "*Deny me this, / And an eternal curse fall on you!*" This shows his arrogance, because he thinks he has power over the Witches.

He remarks that he doesn't care what the Witches need to do to answer his questions, even if "*castles topple on their warders' heads*".

Comment: Macbeth doesn't care about the consequences of his actions on other people. This emphasises his selfish nature.

The Witches agree to answer Macbeth's questions, and summon their masters. The first apparition appears, and it's a head wearing a helmet. The Witches tell Macbeth that he doesn't need to ask his question out loud, the apparition will read his thoughts.

Comment: The apparitions' ability to read Macbeth's mind show their supernatural power.

The first apparition tells Macbeth "*Beware Macduff*".

Comment: The armoured head symbolises Macbeth's beheading at the hands of Macduff.

Act 4, Scene 1 continued

The Witches summon a second apparition, which takes the form of a bloody child. The child tells Macbeth, "*for none of woman born / Shall harm Macbeth.*"

> **Comment:** The second apparition represents Macduff.
>
> The apparition's prediction fills Macbeth with confidence: "*Then live, Macduff. What need I fear of thee?*" He believes that everyone is "*woman born*" so no one can possibly harm him. However, in Act 5, Scene 8 this is proven to be another of the Witches' falsehoods.

The third apparition appears; a child wearing a crown and holding a tree. This apparition tells Macbeth that he won't be defeated until Birnam Wood (a forest near his castle) moves to Dunsinane Hill (a hill near his castle). Macbeth is satisfied that this will never happen as forests can't move.

> **Comment:** The third apparition represents Malcolm. The crown symbolises that he is the rightful king, and the branches represent how he will hide behind branches from Birnam Wood in Act 5, Scene 4.

Finally, Macbeth asks if Banquo's descendants will become king. The Witches summon a procession of eight kings, with the final king holding a mirror in his hand. The line of kings is followed by Banquo. Macbeth recognises that the kings in the procession are Banquo's descendants and is furious. The Witches vanish.

Lennox enters and tells Macbeth that Macduff has fled to England. Macbeth talks to himself and decides to launch an attack on Macduff's castle and kill his wife, children and servants.

Act 4, Scene 2

Lady Macduff asks Ross why her husband has fled to England. She is angry that Macduff has abandoned her and her children: "*He loves us not*". Ross tries to reassure her that Macduff has done the right thing by leaving, telling her that Macduff is "*noble, wise, judicious*".

> **Comment:** Macduff is described as everything that Macbeth is not.

Ross exits, and Lady Macduff is left on stage with her son. A messenger enters and warns Lady Macduff that something dangerous approaches. He begs her to flee with her children. Lady Macduff, panicking, doesn't know where to run.

The murderers enter and stab Lady Macduff's son. She runs off-stage with the murderers following.

> **Comment:** Unlike the previous murders, Macbeth doesn't try to frame anyone for killing the Macduffs. He doesn't even try to disguise his actions.

Act 4, Scene 3

In England, Malcolm and Macduff discuss the sorry state of Scotland. Macduff comments that Scotland has become an awful place where *"New widows howl, new orphans cry."*

> **Comment:** This is another example of dramatic irony. In the previous scene, Macduff's wife and children were murdered.

Malcolm is suspicious that Macduff might be loyal to Macbeth, so he describes himself as lustful and greedy, and confesses he has no qualities, such as *"Devotion, patience, courage, fortitude"*.

> **Comment:** Malcolm presents himself as a terrible ruler to test Macduff. He wants to know if Macduff is loyal to Scotland.

Macduff is outraged by Malcolm's supposed character: *"Fit to govern? / No, not fit to live."* He laments that he will never return to Scotland because Malcolm will be a terrible king. Malcolm confesses that he was testing Macduff to see if Macduff was loyal to Scotland, and that he has passed the test. Malcolm tells Macduff that ten thousand English soldiers are preparing to invade Scotland to win back the crown, and that the King of England, Edward, can perform miracles by curing the sick with his touch. He suggests that Edward's abilities are a gift from God.

> **Comment:** Presenting King Edward as a saintly figure who heals the sick forces the audience to compare him to Macbeth. This makes Macbeth seem even less worthy of being king. For more on King Edward, turn to **page 58**.

Macbeth would have been watched by King James, so Shakespeare would have been careful to praise the English monarchy and present them in a flattering way.

Ross enters and tells Malcolm and Macduff that Scotland is in turmoil, and that *"violent sorrow"* is the only emotion that people know, and that more people are being killed: *"good men's lives, / Expire before the flowers in their caps."*

Macduff asks after his own wife and family. Ross lies and says: *"They're well"*. Macduff senses that he is not being honest and pushes him for the truth.

> **Comment:** Macduff is perceptive, as he knows that Ross is keeping the truth from him. This contrasts with Macbeth who is unable to see through the Witches' dishonesty.

Ross tells Malcolm and Macduff that Macbeth is also preparing an army. He admits that Macduff's castle was invaded, and that his wife and children have been slaughtered. Macduff is distraught.

> **Comment:** Malcolm and Macduff's use of exclamations, e.g. *"Merciful Heaven!"*, shows their shock and anguish at the news. Macduff's grief presents him as a loving husband and father.

Macduff promises to avenge his family's murder and intends to kill Macbeth: *"Bring thou this fiend of Scotland and myself. / Within my sword's length set him."*

ACT 5

This is the final act, and the scenes are relatively short. This increases the pace of the play, which makes it feel as though Macbeth is hurtling towards his fate.

Act 5, Scene 1

A doctor and a gentlewoman (Lady Macbeth's maid) discuss Lady Macbeth. The gentlewoman tells the doctor that she has seen Lady Macbeth sleepwalking.

Comment: The doctor thinks Lady Macbeth's behaviour is unnatural: "*A great perturbation in nature*". This is yet another reference to unnatural events brought about by the Macbeths' actions, such as the horses eating each other in Act 2, Scene 4.

Lady Macbeth enters, sleepwalking. The gentlewoman tells the doctor that Lady Macbeth has been rubbing her hands in her sleep, as if she is trying to wash them.

Comment: Lady Macbeth's sleepwalking and handwashing are signs of her guilt. She's trying to wash imaginary blood from her hands, but she cannot get them clean.

In her sleep, Lady Macbeth implies that she feels responsible for the murder of Macduff's family. "*The thane of Fife had a wife. Where is she now?*"

Lady Macbeth imagines hearing a knocking sound and leaves the stage to go to bed.

Comment: The knocking sound reminds the audience of the knocking sound from Act 2, Scene 2 when Macbeth murdered Duncan.

The doctor thinks that Lady Macbeth can only be cured by a priest.

A painting of Lady Macbeth sleepwalking

The doctor's attitude to Lady Macbeth's psychological illness would have been common at the time. Mental disorders were often thought to have supernatural causes.

Act 5, Scene 2

A group of Scottish nobles, including Angus and Lennox, discuss the situation. The English army, led by Malcolm and Macduff is approaching. Angus remarks they are heading to Birnam Wood.

Comment: This mention of Birnam Wood reminds the audience of the apparition's prediction from Act 4, Scene 1. This hints that Macbeth is about to meet his fate.

The nobles comment on Macbeth's behaviour, as there are rumours that Macbeth has gone mad: *"Some say he's mad"*. Angus implies that he has been driven mad by guilt: *"His secret murders sticking on his hands."*

Comment: This is another reference to guilt and bloody hands.

The nobles decide to switch their allegiance to Malcolm and Macduff.

Act 5, Scene 3

Macbeth has heard that his nobles have abandoned him, but he's still convinced by the apparition's prophecy that no man born of a woman can hurt him.

A servant enters and tells Macbeth that there are ten thousand soldiers marching towards the castle.

Macbeth recognises that this battle will either make his position as king secure, or he will die: *"This push / Will cheer me ever, or disseat me now."* He shows bravery in the face of battle: *"I'll fight till from my bones my flesh be hacked."*

Comment: This reminds the audience of Macbeth the brave warrior from Act 1, Scene 2. His character has come full circle.

The doctor tells Macbeth of his wife's sleepwalking and the visions that trouble her.

Act 5, Scene 4

Malcolm and his men approach Birnam Wood. Malcolm tells the soldiers to cut down a branch and hold it in front of them so that Macbeth's lookouts won't be able to see their movements clearly.

Comment: The audience recognises that the prediction about Birnam Wood coming to Dunsinane Hill will come true, and that Macbeth's fate is sealed.

Act 5, Scene 5

Macbeth waits inside the castle. He believes the advancing army won't be able to enter the castle, and he intends to let the enemy soldiers wait outside until they die of hunger. Macbeth remarks that he would have fought them on the battlefield if so many of his own men hadn't deserted him.

Macbeth hears a woman crying off stage, and Seyton (Macbeth's servant) goes to investigate. He returns, telling Macbeth that Lady Macbeth is dead. Macbeth seems indifferent towards her death: "*She should have died hereafter.*"

Comment: Macbeth's disregard for his wife's death shows just how callous he has become, and contrasts with Macduff's emotional reaction to hearing his wife had died.

A messenger enters and tells Macbeth that he thought he saw Birnam Wood marching towards the castle. Macbeth is angry at the messenger, telling him he will hang him if he's lying, because he knows that this means that he will be defeated.

Macbeth recognises his impending doom, and that he's been deceived by the Witches: "*begin / To doubt th' equivocation of the fiend / That lies like the truth.*"

Comment: Macbeth realised he has been so blinded by his pursuit of power that he has been fooled by the Witches.

Macbeth decides to leave the castle to fight. He's realised that he's fated to die, and he wants to get it over with: "*I 'gin to be aweary of the sun.*"

Act 5, Scene 6

Malcolm, Macduff and their army approach Macbeth's caslte. Malcolm instructs his men to throw down the branches they have been using to hide themselves.

Act 5, Scene 7

Macbeth comments that he feels like a bear tied to a stake. He's prepared to fight but he feels restricted and vulnerable.

> **Comment:** Bear-baiting was a common blood sport in the 17th century. A bear would be tied to a stake and attacked by a pack of dogs. People would watch the animals fight to the death as a form of entertainment. This reflects how the audience watching *Macbeth* are also watching a fight to the death as a form of entertainment.

Young Siward (a general in the English army, and son of Old Siward) enters and fights Macbeth. Young Siward is killed. Macbeth feels confident again, repeating the apparition's prophecy that he cannot be killed by a man who is woman born.

> **Comment:** Macbeth exits, then Macduff enters and exits, followed by Malcolm and Old Siward. The characters entering and exiting the stage mimics the confusion and chaos of battle.

Act 5, Scene 8

Macbeth contemplates killing himself, but resolves to kill his enemies instead. Macduff enters, and challenges Macbeth to fight.

> **Comment:** Macduff calls Macbeth a "*hellhound*". This dehumanises him, and this demonic image contrasts with the saintly imagery used to describe the other kings, Duncan and Edward.

Macbeth confesses that Macduff is the only person he is afraid of: "*Of all men else I have avoided thee.*" They fight and Macbeth taunts Macduff telling him that he can't be hurt by any man who is born of a woman. Macduff tells Macbeth that he was delivered by caesarean. Macbeth realises that he has been deceived by the Witches yet again: "*And be these juggling fiends no more believed.*"

> **Comment:** The audience realises the true meaning of the apparition's final prophecy at the same time as Macbeth.

Macbeth and Macduff fight, and Macduff kills Macbeth.

Malcolm, Ross and Siward enter. They discuss how Young Siward died bravely in battle. Macduff enters with Macbeth's head. They all hail Malcolm, the new King of Scotland.

CHARACTERS: MACBETH

Macbeth is the play's **protagonist**. His character is complex, and he changes throughout the course of the play.

Act 1

Brave: Before he even appears on stage, the other characters speak of Macbeth's bravery. *"For brave Macbeth—well he deserves that name."*

Comment: Shakespeare presents Macbeth as brave and heroic at the start of the play. This makes his descent into tyranny more shocking.

Violent: In Act 1, Scene 2, Macbeth is reported to have sliced a man in half and hung the man's head on the walls of the castle. *"Till he unseamed him from the nave to th' chops, / And fixed his head upon our battlements."*

Macbeth is a brave warrior at the start of the play

Comment: Although the other characters think this is "*valiant*" (heroic) behaviour, it's the audience's first hint that Macbeth isn't afraid to kill. However, the men that Macbeth kills on the battlefield do not affect his conscience in the same way as Duncan and Banquo.

Ambitious: When the Witches make the prophecy about Macbeth becoming king, he immediately thinks about killing Duncan: "*My thought, whose murder yet is but fantastical*".

Comment: This demonstrates that Macbeth is prepared to do anything to become king.

Uncertain: Although he contemplates murdering Duncan, he still has doubts. Thinking about murder "*Shakes so my single state of man*".

Comment: At this point, Macbeth still has a conscience and recognises that murder is wrong. This attitude changes as the play progresses.

In Act 1, Scene 3, Macbeth speaks to himself several times. This hints at his deceptive behaviour, as he's hiding his true thoughts from Banquo.

Act 1, Scene 5

Lady Macbeth reveals a lot about her husband in her soliloquy at the very start of Act 1, Scene 5. She acknowledges that Macbeth "*Art not without ambition*", but she is concerned that he is "*too full o' th' milk of human kindness*" to realise his true potential. She believes that Macbeth is too honourable, commenting that he "*wouldst not play false*". This suggests that Macbeth was an honourable man before he is corrupted by his ambition.

Act 2

Indecisive: Although he has considered killing Duncan, Macbeth initially decides against it: "*We will proceed no further in this business.*"

> **Comment:** Macbeth's indecisiveness shows the fight between his ambition and his conscience. At this point, his conscience is overruling his ambition.

Easily manipulated: Lady Macbeth convinces Macbeth to kill Duncan by calling him a coward and questioning his masculinity: "*And live a coward in thine own esteem.*"

> **Comment:** Bravery is an important aspect of Macbeth's character, so by questioning his courage, Lady Macbeth can manipulate Macbeth.

Frightened: After Macbeth kills Duncan, he is terrified by what he has done. He forgets to smear the sleeping servants with blood, and he refuses to go back to plant the daggers: "*I'll go no more: / I am afraid to think what I have done; / Look on 't again I dare not.*"

> **Comment:** Duncan's murder has changed Macbeth. He's no longer the fearless warrior from Act 1, Scene 2.

Remorseful: Macbeth feels remorse for killing Duncan. "*Wake Duncan with thy knocking. I wish thou couldst.*"

> **Comment:** Even though he's done something terrible, Macbeth still has a conscience and feels guilt. He's not yet become a monster.

Act 3

Troubled: Duncan's murder has given him nightmares: "*In the affliction of these terrible dreams / That shake us nightly.*"

> **Comment:** This suggests that Macbeth feels regret for what he has done, and still has a conscience. This contrasts with his lack of remorse for the murders of the Macduffs in Act 4.

Insecure: Macbeth is paranoid about Banquo and the prediction that Banquo's descendants will be kings. He decides to hire murderers to kill Banquo and his son, Fleance.

> **Comment:** Lady Macbeth had to convince Macbeth to kill Duncan, but Macbeth decides to kill Banquo and Fleance of his own accord, suggesting that he is now acting independently, rather than being influenced by his wife.

Guilty: Macbeth's guilt at killing Banquo manifests as the ghost of Banquo.

> **Comment:** Macbeth is terrified by the ghost. This contrasts with Macbeth's portrayal as a brave warrior in Act 1, Scene 2.

Act 4

Easily manipulated: Macbeth visits the Witches in Act 4, Scene 1. They easily deceive him with ambiguous prophecies from the apparitions, which fill Macbeth with false confidence: *"Sweet bodements! Good! / Rebellious dead, rise never till the wood / Of Birnam rise."*

> **Comment:** Macbeth's ambition and desire for power clouds his judgement. He believes everything the Witches tell him.

Tyrannical: After visiting the Witches, Macbeth decides to have Macduff's family killed. *"give to th' edge o' th' sword / His wife, his babes, and all unfortunate souls."*

Macbeth becomes a tyrannical king

> **Comment:** Macbeth's transformation into a tyrant is now complete. He's prepared to kill women and children. Unlike the murder of Duncan, he doesn't debate these killings, instead he sees them as essential for maintaining his power.

Act 5

Erratic: By Act 5, Macbeth is consumed by his feelings of guilt and his behaviour becomes increasingly erratic. He mutters to himself and pulls his armour on and off.

Heartless: In Act 5, Scene 5, the doctor tells Macbeth that his wife is dead, but Macbeth's reaction is cold: *"She should have died hereafter."*

> **Comment:** In Act 1, Scene 5, Macbeth speaks tenderly to his wife. He calls her his *"dearest partner in greatness"* and *"My dearest love"*. The affection that they once had for each other has been destroyed.

Cynical: When a messenger tells Macbeth that he has seen Birnam Wood move towards the castle, Macbeth becomes enraged, but this fury quickly turns to cynicism. *"I 'gin to be aweary of the sun"*.

> **Comment:** At this point, Macbeth has realised that the apparitions' prophecies are coming true and his own fate is out of his hands.

Brave: Although Macbeth is resigned to his fate, he wants to fight with courage. He comments that he will fight *"bearlike"*.

> **Comment:** Macbeth's character has come full circle. He's returned to the brave warrior of Act 1.

Read the following extract from Act 1, Scene 3 of *Macbeth*. At this point in the play, Macbeth has just discovered he has been given the title Thane of Cawdor.

MACBETH

[aside] This supernatural soliciting
Cannot be ill, cannot be good. If ill,
Why hath it given me earnest of success,
Commencing in a truth? I am thane of Cawdor.
If good, why do I yield to that suggestion
Whose horrid image doth unfix my hair
And make my seated heart knock at my ribs,
Against the use of nature? Present fears
Are less than horrible imaginings.
My thought, whose murder yet is but fantastical,
Shakes so my single state of man
That function is smother'd in surmise,
And nothing is but what is not.

BANQUO

Look, how our partner's rapt.

MACBETH

[aside] If chance will have me king, why, chance may crown me
Without my stir

> ⭐ Use the introductory sentences above the extract to help you identify where in the play the extract is taken from. This will help you to think about the play as a whole.

Starting with this speech, explore how far Shakespeare presents Macbeth as an ambitious character.

Write about:
- How Shakespeare presents Macbeth in this extract
- How far Shakespeare presents Macbeth as an ambitious character in the play as a whole

[30 + 4 marks]

Your answer may include:

AO1 — show understanding of the text
- Macbeth realises that the prophecies are real and starts to believe he could become king. This scene is the audience's first hint of Macbeth's ambitious nature.
- He is doubtful about the Witches' intentions: "Cannot be ill, cannot be good." His ambition hasn't completely blinded him to the Witches' deception yet. This contrasts with later in the play where he is easily manipulated by the Witches because of his desire for power.
- Macbeth considers murdering Duncan to fulfil his ambition, but the thoughts terrify him: "make my seated heart knock at my ribs." He still has a conscience.
- Macbeth recognises that he might become king without taking any action: "chance may crown me / Without my stir." This contrasts with later in the play where kills without conscience to keep his power.
- Macbeth is a tragedy, and protagonists in tragedies often have a fatal flaw. Ambition is Macbeth's fatal flaw which causes him to kill Duncan, Banquo and the Macduffs, and ultimately ends in his own downfall.

AO2 — show understanding of the writer's language choices
- Shakespeare's use of rhetorical questions emphasises Macbeth's uncertainty and the conflict between his conscience and his ambition.
- Phrase "knock at my ribs" foreshadows the knocking noise after Duncan is killed.
- This soliloquy spoken as an aside is used to show Macbeth's innermost thoughts and how he is conflicted about killing Duncan. This contrasts with later murders where Macbeth doesn't debate whether he should kill Banquo and the Macduffs. His ambition overpowers his conscience.

AO3 — relate the play to the context
- 17th-century audiences would have recognised the Witches as evil characters who bring misfortune on others. Macbeth's ambition for power blinds him to this.
- Regicide was seen as a crime against God because of the belief in the Divine Right of Kings. Macbeth's ambition means he is prepared to provoke God.

This answer should be marked in accordance with the levels-based mark scheme on pages 61..

Make sure your answer to this question is in paragraphs and full sentences. Bullet points have been used in this example answer to suggest some information you could include. There are four marks available for spelling, punctuation and grammar, so make sure you read through your answer carefully, correcting any mistakes.

CHARACTERS: LADY MACBETH

Lady Macbeth would have shocked Shakespearian audiences. They would have expected a lady to be gentle, submissive and kind.

Act 1

Manipulative: When Lady Macbeth reads the letter about the prophecies, she urges Macbeth to return home quickly so that she can manipulate him. *"Hie thee hither, / That I may pour my spirits in thine ear."*

Comment: Lady Macbeth knows that she can influence her husband, suggesting that she has done this before. Referencing *"spirits"* here (and again in Act 1, Scene 5) links Lady Macbeth to the Witches and the theme of the supernatural.

Deceitful: Lady Macbeth welcomes Duncan to her castle and flatters him, even though she intends to kill him.

Comment: Lady Macbeth's deception reminds the audience of the Witches' comment that *"Fair is foul"*.

Lady Macbeth manipulates her husband to achieve her own ambitions.

Ambitious: At the start of the play, Lady Macbeth is arguably more ambitious than her husband. She convinces Macbeth to murder Duncan, even when he has decided against it.

Comment: She thinks that women are too gentle to commit murder, so she remarks, *"unsex me here"*. Lady Macbeth wants to reject her femininity so that she can kill Duncan. Lady Macbeth taunts her husband's masculinity to get what she wants: *"Be so much more the man"*.

Ruthless: Lady Macbeth comments if she had sworn to dash *"the brains out"* of her own child *"while it was smiling in my face"* she would have kept her promise.

Comment: The image of infanticide (killing an infant) is horrific. This presents Lady Macbeth as unnatural and monstrous.

Act 2

Fearless: Lady Macbeth returns to the scene of the murder to smear the servants with blood and plant the dagger to frame them for Duncan's murder. This shows her boldness, especially since Macbeth refused to do it.

> **Comment:** Even though Lady Macbeth doesn't kill Duncan herself, smearing the servants with blood causes her to literally have blood on her hands. This symbolises that she is just as responsible for Duncan's death as Macbeth.

Dominant: Lady Macbeth repeatedly taunts and bullies her husband: *"My hands are of your colour, but I shame / To wear a heart so white."*

> **Comment:** Lady Macbeth's dominance over her husband would have been shocking to 17th-century audiences as her control in the marriage would have gone against typical gender roles of that period.

Clever: After Duncan's body is found, Macbeth confesses to killing Duncan's servants out of rage. Lady Macbeth faints, possibly to divert attention from what Macbeth is saying, in case people become suspicious of his actions.

> **Comment:** Women were thought to be more delicate and more prone to fainting, so Lady Macbeth uses preconceptions about her femininity to deceive the other characters.

Act 3

Remorseful: Lady Macbeth shows signs of remorse in Act 3: *"Tis safer to be that which we destroy / Than by destruction dwell in doubtful joy."*

> **Comment:** This is a turning point for Lady Macbeth and signals the beginning of the guilt that will eventually send her mad.

Dominant: In Act 3, Scene 4 where Macbeth sees Banquo's ghost at the feast, Lady Macbeth reprimands Macbeth for causing a scene: *"Shame itself! / Why do you make such faces?"*

Act 5

Disturbed: By Act 5, Lady Macbeth has been driven mad by guilt. She is sleepwalking and scrubbing her hands, trying to wash away imaginary blood.

> **Comment:** Lady Macbeth's speech in Act 5, Scene 1 is fragmented and repetitive: *"To bed, to bed. There's knocking at the gate. Come, / come, come, come."* This shows how disturbed and tortured her mind is.

Dead: Lady Macbeth commits suicide in Scene 5. Seyton announces: *"The queen, my lord, is dead"*. She is so overcome by guilt that she kills herself.

Read the following extract from Act 1, Scene 7 of *Macbeth*. At this point in the play, Macbeth tells his wife that he has decided not to murder Duncan.

MACBETH

> We will proceed no further in this business.
> He hath honoured me of late, and I have bought
> Golden opinions from all sorts of people,
> Which would be worn in their newest gloss,
> Not cast aside so soon.

LADY MACBETH

> Was the hope drunk
> Wherein you dressed yourself? Hath it slept since?
> And wakes it now, to look so green and pale
> At what it did so freely? From this time
> Such I account thy love. Art thou afeard
> To be the same in thine own act and valour
> As thou art in desire? Wouldst thou have that
> Which thou esteem'st the ornament of life,
> And live a coward in thine own esteem,
> Letting "I dare not" wait upon "I would",
> Like the poor cat i' th' adage?

MACBETH

> Prithee, peace:
> I dare do all that may become a man;
> Who dares do more is none.

⭐ Use the introductory sentences above the extract to help you identify where in the play the extract is taken from. This will help you to think about the play as a whole.

Starting with this moment in the play, explore how far Shakespeare presents Lady Macbeth as a controlling character.

Write about:
- How Shakespeare presents Lady Macbeth in this extract
- How far Shakespeare presents Lady Macbeth as a controlling character in the play as a whole.

[30 + 4 marks]

Your answer may include:

AO1 — show understanding of the text
- *In the first three acts, Lady Macbeth tries to control her husband, attempting to emotionally blackmail him or taunt his masculinity, in order to provoke him into doing what she wants.*
- *In Act 2, Scene 2, she takes control of planting evidence at Duncan's murder scene after Macbeth refuses to do it. She mocks Macbeth, calling him a coward: "My hands are of your colour, but I shame / To wear a heart so white."*
- *By Act 3, Lady Macbeth starts to have less control over Macbeth. He decides to kill Banquo without her involvement: "Be innocent of the knowledge". This suggests that her control over him is weakening. However, in Act 3, Scene 4 when Macbeth is terrified by the ghost of Banquo, Lady Macbeth again tries to control him by questioning his masculinity, saying it is "A woman's story at a winter's fire". Lady Macbeth is barely able to control her husband's outbursts, and his actions lead the nobles at the feast to become suspicious of him.*
- *Lady Macbeth doesn't appear in Act 4, and by Act 5 Scene 1 she has been driven mad, and no longer has any control over Macbeth's actions.*

AO2 — show understanding of the writer's language choices
- *Lady Macbeth repeatedly uses rhetorical questions in this extract to taunt and provoke her husband. "Hath it slept since?".*
- *When Macbeth decides against killing Duncan ("We will proceed no further in this business.") Lady Macbeth questions Macbeth's love for her: "From this time / Such I account thy love." She uses emotional blackmail to try to control him.*
- *Lady Macbeth also taunts him, calling him a "coward". Since Macbeth is presented as a brave warrior earlier in the play, she knows that mocking his courage will provoke him into doing what she wants. Her provocation works, as Macbeth eventually kills Duncan.*

AO3 — relate the play to the context
- *Lady Macbeth's control over Macbeth would have gone against typical gender roles in the 17th century where women were supposed to be weak and subservient. Lady Macbeth's control over her husband would have shocked 17th-century audiences.*

This answer should be marked in accordance with the levels-based mark scheme on pages 61.

> Make sure your answer to this question is in paragraphs and full sentences. Bullet points have been used in this example answer to suggest some information you could include. There are four marks available for spelling, punctuation and grammar, so make sure you read through your answer carefully, correcting any mistakes.

CHARACTERS: BANQUO

Banquo possesses all the noble qualities that Macbeth doesn't. Unfortunately, his honourable nature gets him killed.

King James I claimed to be descended from Banquo, so Shakespeare portrays Banquo in a positive way to flatter the king.

Banquo acts as a **foil** to Macbeth. See **page 11** for more.

Act 1

Brave: Banquo fights bravely on the battlefield. The bloodied captain tells Duncan that Banquo and Macbeth seemed as afraid of battle as *"sparrows eagles, or the hare the lion."*

Cautious: He is wary of the Witches' predictions and believes that the Witches intend to deceive to cause harm: *"Win us with honest trifles, to betray 's / In deepest consequences."*

Comment: He is suspicious of the Witches' intentions and less easily deceived than Macbeth.

Like Macbeth, Banquo is a brave warrior.

Act 2

Restrained: Banquo admits he has dreamt about the prophecies and doing terrible things to make them come true: *"Restrain in me the cursèd thoughts that nature / Gives way to in repose."*

Comment: Although he is tempted to do terrible things to make the prophecies come true, unlike Macbeth, he resists. Banquo represents an alternative course of action.

Honourable: Macbeth implies that if Banquo supports him in the future, he will be rewarded. Banquo agrees he will support Macbeth provided it doesn't bring him dishonour. *"but still keep / My bosom franchised and allegiance clear."*

Comment: Unlike Macbeth, Banquo prizes honour above his ambition. However, his reluctance to act dishonourably probably seals his fate.

Act 3

Suspicious: Banquo suspects Macbeth is responsible for Duncan's murder: *"I fear / Thou played'st most foully for 't"*.

Comment: Although he is perceptive enough to suspect Macbeth, Banquo is naïve to think he isn't in any danger. Just like Duncan, he is deceived by Macbeth's flattery (*"Here's our chief guest"*) before he is killed by the hired murderers.

Banquo is the only murdered character to reappear as a ghost. This suggests that Macbeth feels especially guilty for killing him.

CHARACTERS: DUNCAN

Duncan is the King of Scotland. He only appears in Act 1, and is killed off-stage by Macbeth in Act 2.

Act 1

Trusting: Duncan is very trusting. He never suspected that the Thane of Cawdor would betray him, and he trusts the Macbeths when he visits their castle.

Comment: Duncan's trusting nature leads to his downfall. Shakespeare could be commenting that being too trusting is a bad quality for a king to have. For more on the theme of kingship, turn to **page 56**.

Generous: Duncan is a generous king. He rewards those who serve him well. He gives Macbeth the title of Thane of Cawdor for his victory in battle.

Comment: Duncan's generosity suggests that Macbeth could have gained more titles and power through loyal service, and that he could have become king without murdering Duncan.

Duncan is presented as an ideal king.

Grateful: He appreciates Macbeth's service. *"More is thy duty than more than all can pay."*

Comment: Shakespeare presents Duncan as a likeable character. This makes his murder more shocking, and the Macbeths' betrayal seem even worse.

Sensitive: Duncan isn't afraid to show his emotions: *"My plenteous joys, Wanton in fullness, seek to hide themselves / In drops of sorrow."*

Comment: The characters who show their emotions, such as Macduff and Malcolm in Act 4, Scene 3, are also strong, honourable characters. Shakespeare hints that showing grief and emotion does not make someone weak.

Duncan's compassionate and benevolent leadership contrasts with the tyranny of Macbeth's rule later in the play which is described as *"Devilish"*. The audience recognises that Macbeth doesn't want to be king because he thinks he can do a better job than Duncan: he wants to be king for his own selfish ambition.

Although Duncan is presented as a kind-hearted king, he does condemn the Thane of Cawdor to death for treason, so he's not completely forgiving.

CHARACTERS: THE WITCHES

The Witches only appear in four scenes, but their actions drive the whole play and bring about Macbeth's downfall. Unlike some of the other characters, they don't change or develop, they're evil and vindictive throughout.

Act 1

Comment: The Witches speak in rhyming couplets. This gives their lines a sing-song quality which mimics the casting of a spell. They often speak in **trochaic tetrameter** (see **page 9**) which contrasts with the iambic pentameter used by the other characters.

Vindictive: The Witches use their powers for revenge. They curse a sailor because the sailor's wife wouldn't give them some chestnuts.

Comment: This shows how petty the Witches are and demonstrates what they are capable of.

The Witches are one of several supernatural elements in the play (see page 50 for more).

Powerful: The Witches summon a storm for 81 days.

Comment: The storm they summon in Act 1, Scene 3 foreshadows the storm the night of Duncan's murder. This suggests that they might be responsible for that storm too.

Cryptic: They speak in riddles and use antithesis when talking to Macbeth and Banquo: *"Lesser than Macbeth and greater."*

Comment: They deliberately make their speech unclear so they can mislead Macbeth.

Shakespeare's portrayal of the Witches would have drawn on common perceptions about witchcraft. During the 16th and 17th centuries, witches were often blamed for a person's misfortune, for example, illness, poor harvests and bad weather.

Act 4

Unpleasant: The Witches concoct a potion made from hideous ingredients, including a dead baby's finger and *"Nose of Turk"*.

Comment: It's never revealed why the Witches have chosen to manipulate Macbeth, and what their motivations are. In Act 4, Scene 1, Hecate says: *"I command your pains, / And every one shall share i' th' gains."* This implies that the Witches will benefit from Macbeth's downfall in some way, but this is never revealed.

CHARACTERS: MACDUFF

Macduff puts his love for Scotland before everything else, even his wife and children. Macduff's loyalty to his country contrasts with Macbeth's selfishness.

Act 2

Suspicious: Macduff doesn't attend Macbeth's coronation. This deliberate snub suggests that he is suspicious of Macbeth, and doesn't support him becoming king.

Act 3

Honourable: Macduff goes to England to raise an army to overthrow Macbeth and restore the rightful king to the throne. Unlike Macbeth, Macduff doesn't want power for himself, he just wants a good and legitimate king to rule Scotland.

> **Comment:** The other Lords, such as Lennox and Ross, are hesitant to act against Macbeth initially. Macduff's decision to go to England to raise an army without the support of his fellow nobles shows his bravery and loyalty to his country.

Stubborn: Macbeth sends a messenger to request that Macduff return to Scotland but Macduff refuses. The messenger threatens Macduff: "*You'll rue the time / That clogs me with this answer.*"

Macduff becomes the focus of Macbeth's insecurity.

> **Comment:** Macduff's refusal to return to Scotland shows his naivety because he doesn't recognise how dangerous Macbeth is, which leads to the death of his family.

> Macduff is the play's **antagonist**. An antagonist is the main foe to the **protagonist**.

Act 4

> **Comment:** The first apparition tells Macbeth "*Beware Macduff*". This encourages Macbeth to send the murderers to kill Macduff's family.

Honest: When Malcolm pretends to be a bad leader in Act 4, Scene 3, Macduff despairs. "*Fit to govern? / No, not to live.*" Unlike the thanes that surround Macbeth and don't stand up to him, Macduff is prepared to speak out against tyranny.

Loving: When Macduff discovers his family has been slaughtered, he is devastated. Macduff's grief contrasts with Macbeth's lack of emotion when Lady Macbeth dies.

> **Comment:** Shakespeare repeatedly uses questions to show Macduff's shock and disbelief: "*All my pretty ones? / Did you say all? O hell-kite! All?*"

Vengeful: Macduff vows to avenge his family's death: "*Front to front / Bring thou this fiend of Scotland any myself. / Within my sword's length set him.*"

CHARACTERS: MALCOLM AND DONALBAIN

Malcolm and Donalbain are Duncan's sons. They flee Scotland after Macbeth murders their father, but return in Act 5 with an army, ready for revenge.

Act 2

Wary: After Duncan's body is discovered, Malcolm and Donalbain recognise that they are in danger: "*Where we are, / There's daggers in men's smiles.*"

> **Comment:** Malcolm and Donalbain are more perceptive than Duncan and realise that they shouldn't trust the thanes.

Patient: They're both upset by their father's death, but they agree not to do anything reckless to avenge him straight away: "*Nor our strong sorrow / Upon the foot of motion.*"

> **Comment:** Malcolm and Donalbain's caution and patience contrasts with Macbeth's recklessness. This suggests that they will be far better leaders than Macbeth.

When Malcolm and Donalbain flee Scotland, this makes them the main suspects for Duncan's murder. Their absence allows Macbeth to become king instead.

Act 4

Wary: When Macduff visits Malcolm in England, Malcolm is wary. He's suspicious of Macduff and thinks he could have been sent by Macbeth to betray him. He pretends to be a terrible person to test Malcolm: "*had I power, I should / Pour the sweet milk of concord into hell.*"

Virtuous: Malcolm tells Macduff he "*Scarcely coveted what was mine own, / At no time broke my faith, would not betray / The devil to his fellow.*" He's never broken a vow, barely cares about his own possessions, has never broken a promise and wouldn't even betray the devil.

> **Comment:** Malcolm says he's not greedy, is God-fearing and wouldn't even betray the devil. These qualities suggest he's the exact opposite to Macbeth. This implies he will be a good ruler. For more on the theme of kingship, turn to **page 56**.

Act 5

Cunning: Malcolm suggests that the army hold branches in front on them to disguise their approach to Macbeth's castle.

> **Comment:** The apparition Macbeth sees with the crown and the branch in Act 4, Scene 1 symbolises Malcolm.

Generous: After Macbeth is defeated, Malcolm rewards his loyal followers: "*My thanes and kinsmen, / Henceforth be earls.*"

> **Comment:** This generosity reminds the audience of Duncan, and suggests that Malcolm will be a generous king.

THEMES: AMBITION

The Macbeths' ambition drives the action of the play.

Macbeth

Ambition is Macbeth's **fatal flaw**: the characteristic that brings about his downfall. At the beginning of the play, he is portrayed as loyal to King Duncan (he is fighting against an invading army on Duncan's behalf) and a heroic warrior, but the Witches' prophecies turn him into a power-hungry tyrant.

Macbeth's ambition blinds him to the truth, and his desire for power means he is easily manipulated by the Witches throughout the play. He's so desperate to believe their prophecies he ignores their wicked nature and overlooks their deliberately ambiguous language. Where Banquo is wary of the prophecies and declines to act, Macbeth turns to murder.

The Macbeths' ambition ultimately leads to their downfall.

Comment: Banquo is tempted by ambition when the Witches prophesise his descendants will become king. He has "*cursèd thoughts*" but he doesn't act on the prophecies because he values his honour over his ambition.

Macbeth's ambition does not stop when he becomes king. He is so desperate to keep his power that he has Banquo murdered to try to stop Banquo's descendants from becoming king, and he kills the Macduffs because the apparition tells him: "*Beware Macduff.*" Eventually, Macbeth's ambition leads to his own death.

Comment: Even though he gets what he wants, Macbeth is never satisfied. Shakespeare could be warning the audience about the dangers of "*Vaulting ambition*".

Lady Macbeth

Lady Macbeth is ambitious, arguably even more so than her husband. In Act 1, Scene 5, Lady Macbeth fears that Macbeth doesn't have the strength of character to make his ambitions a reality: "*Art not without ambition, but without / The illness should attend it*" and decides to manipulate Macbeth into acting on his ambition.

Comment: Without Lady Macbeth's manipulation, Macbeth might not have killed Duncan. It could be argued that it's Lady Macbeth's ambition that sets Macbeth on a path to destruction.

Lady Macbeth's ambition appears to stop at becoming queen, as she isn't involved in the murder of Banquo or the Macduffs. However, Duncan's murder and her knowledge of the other murders eventually sends her mad and results in her death.

Read the following extract from Act 1, Scene 5. At this point in the play, Lady Macbeth has just read a letter from Macbeth, telling her about the Witches' prophecies.

LADY MACBETH

> Glamis thou art, and Cawdor; and shalt be
>
> What thou art promised. Yet do I fear thy nature;
>
> It is too full o' the' milk of human kindness
>
> To catch the nearest way: thou wouldst be great,
>
> Art not without ambition, but without
>
> The illness should attend it. What thou wouldst highly,
>
> That wouldst thou holily; wouldst not play false,
>
> And yet wouldst wrongly win. Thou'ld'st have, great Glamis,
>
> That which cries, "Thou must do," if thou have it,
>
> And that which rather thou dost fear to do,
>
> Than wishest should be undone. Hie thee hither,
>
> That I may pour my spirits in thine ear
>
> And chastise with the valour of my tongue
>
> All that impedes thee from the golden round,
>
> Which fate and metaphysical aid doth seem
>
> To have crowned withal

> ⭐ Use the introductory sentences above the extract to help you identify where in the play the extract is taken from. This will help you to think about the play as a whole.

Starting with this speech, explore how Shakespeare presents the theme of ambition.

Write about:
- How Shakespeare presents ambition in this extract
- How far Shakespeare presents ambition in the play as a whole

[30 + 4 marks]

Your answer may include:

AO1 — show understanding of the text
- Lady Macbeth recognises they have been given an opportunity to become more powerful, and unlike Macbeth, she isn't wary of the Witches' prediction. Her ambition clouds her judgement.
- Lady Macbeth acknowledges that Macbeth is ambitious: "Art not without ambition" but she is concerned that he doesn't have the strength of character to realise his ambitions "thy nature; / It is too full o' the' milk of human kindness." This description of Macbeth indicates that he was a good person before he became corrupted by ambition.
- Lady Macbeth is presented as the more ambitious character here, as she intends to manipulate him: "Hie thee hither, / That I may pour my spirits in thine ear."
- Later in the play, their roles are reversed, and Macbeth becomes the more ambitious character as he kills Banquo and the Macduffs without his wife's involvement.
- Shakespeare uses the play to warn against the dangers of ambition. The characters who act on their ambition are never satisfied, and their ambition only seems to bring them misery, and ultimately, their downfall.

AO2 — show understanding of the writer's language choices
- Shakespeare uses this soliloquy to present Lady Macbeth's ambitious nature to the audience.
- Lady Macbeth's reference to "spirits" connects her with the Witches, which suggests her ambition might be evil.

AO3 — relate the play to the context
- Lady Macbeth's ambition would be shocking to 17th-century audiences, as women were seen as weak and gentle.
- 17th-century audiences would have interpreted the Witches as evil characters, and recognised that their prophecies intend to cause harm.

This answer should be marked in accordance with the levels-based mark scheme on pages 61.

Make sure your answer to this question is in paragraphs and full sentences. Bullet points have been used in this example answer to suggest some information you could include. There are four marks available for spelling, punctuation and grammar, so make sure you read through your answer carefully, correcting any mistakes.

THEMES: SUPERNATURAL

As well as being a theme, the supernatural is also a structural device. It drives Macbeth's actions throughout the course of the play.

Context of the supernatural

The supernatural elements in *Macbeth* are presented as evil and unnatural. This may be because of King James' negative attitude towards witchcraft, and the panic surrounding witch hunts in the 17th century (see **page 4**). Seventeenth-century audiences would have been both fearful and fascinated by the supernatural.

Comment: The supernatural elements in the play present an opportunity to create a spectacle for the audience. The Witches may have entered the stage via a trapdoor in the floor to show that they have travelled up from Hell.

King James wrote a book about witchcraft in 1597 called *Daemonologie*.

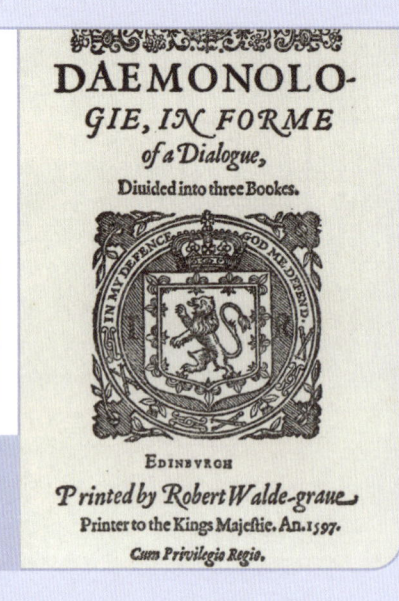

The Witches and Hecate

The Witches and Hecate are the most recognisable supernatural elements in the play. The Witches are very powerful; they can predict the future, summon storms and vanish into thin air. They use their powers for evil, either to get revenge (i.e. the sailor in Act 1, Scene 3) or to manipulate and control (i.e. Macbeth). The portrayal of the Witches would have reflected 17th-century attitudes towards witchcraft: malevolent forces used to torment and bring misfortune.

Comment: Although the Witches have supernatural powers, it's their ability to exploit and manipulate Macbeth that makes them dangerous. The Witches don't harm any of the characters in the play directly; the murders are all committed by Macbeth.

The Witches are associated with stormy weather, and they enter the stage to "*Thunder and lightning*". This suggests that the Witches are linked to disturbances in the natural world.

Comment: Shakespeare warns the audience against getting involved in witchcraft, suggesting that the supernatural will only ever bring misfortune.

The Witches are described as having "*beards*", which gives their characters a masculine quality, and implies that they will not have the characteristics stereotypically associated with women at that time: kindness, weakness and subservience.

The ghostly dagger

The ghostly dagger that Macbeth sees in Act 2, Scene 1 is a dramatic device which shows how supernatural forces have overcome Macbeth. It's not clear whether the dagger is real, or just a figment of Macbeth's imagination. The dagger draws Macbeth towards Duncan, and its presence encourages Macbeth to go through with the murder.

Some productions of *Macbeth* show the ghostly dagger on-stage, while others do not.

The ghost of Banquo

Banquo is the only murdered character to come back as a ghost. Like the ghostly dagger, it's unclear whether the ghost is real, or just a hallucination since only Macbeth can see him. The appearance of the ghost suggests murdering Banquo weighs heavily on Macbeth's conscience, and symbolises how the supernatural continues to torment him.

Comment: The ghost of Banquo sits in Macbeth's chair. This represents how Banquo's descendants will ultimately replace Macbeth as king.

The apparitions

In Act 4, Scene 1, the Witches summon three apparitions to answer Macbeth's questions: an armoured head, a bloodied child and a child wearing a crown holding a branch. The three apparitions symbolise Macbeth's downfall: the armoured head represents his beheading; the bloodied child represents Macduff, and the child with a crown represents Malcolm holding the branches of Birnam Wood. It's ironic that Macbeth cannot see his own undoing even when the Witches present it to him in the form of the apparitions. This shows just how blinded by ambition he has become.

Read the following extract from Act 4, Scene 1 of *Macbeth*. At this point in the play, Macbeth has gone to see the Witches to ask them to answer his questions.

SECOND WITCH

    By the pricking of my thumbs,

    Something wicked this way comes.

    Open, locks,

    Whoever knocks.

MACBETH enters.

MACBETH

    How now, you secret, black, and midnight hags?

    What is 't you do?

ALL

    A deed without a name.

MACBETH

    I conjure you by that which you profess—

    Howe'er you come to know it—answer me.

    Though you untie the winds and let them fight

    Against the churches, though the yeasty waves

    Confound and swallow navigation up,

    Though bladed corn be lodged and trees blown down,

    Though castles topple on their warders' heads,

    Though palaces and pyramids do slope

    Their heads to their foundations, though the treasure

    Of nature's germens tumble all together,

    Even till destruction sicken, answer me

    To what I ask you

> Use the introductory sentences above the extract to help you identify where in the play the extract is taken from. This will help you to think about the play as a whole.

Starting with this speech, explore how Shakespeare presents the attitude of Macbeth towards the supernatural.

Write about:
- How Shakespeare presents the attitude of Macbeth towards the supernatural in this extract
- How far Shakespeare presents the attitudes of Macbeth towards the supernatural in the play as a whole

[30 + 4 marks]

Your answer may include:

AO1 — show understanding of the text
- Macbeth realises that Witches are powerful. He knows they can "untie the winds".
- Macbeth recognises that the Witches are evil, but he doesn't care about the consequences of their actions on others: "Though castles toppled on their warders' heads". He only cares how the Witches' powers can benefit him.
- This extract shows Macbeth's arrogance towards the supernatural. Even though the Witches are powerful and dangerous, Macbeth demands answers from them.
- Macbeth is reliant on the Witches. He actively seeks them out to hear their predictions and to reassure himself. The Witches' predictions cause Macbeth to have false confidence.

AO2 — show understanding of the writer's language choices
- Macbeth uses demanding language to try to control the Witches. He repeats the phrase "answer me".
- The destructive imagery of castles crumbling, shipwrecks and trees being blown down suggests that Macbeth has a negative attitude towards the supernatural and sees it as evil.
- The supernatural is used as a structural device to drive the plot. The Witches' predictions in Act 1, drive the plot in the first half of the play. This scene drives the action in Acts 4 and 5.

AO3 — relate the play to the context
- 17th-century audiences would have recognised the Witches as evil characters who bring misfortune on others. This portrayal would have supported their attitudes.
- 17th-century audiences would have been fearful and fascinated by the supernatural.
- Shakespeare uses the play to warn against getting involved in witchcraft, implying that it will only bring misery.
- The supernatural elements in the play would have been a dramatic spectacle for the audience.

This answer should be marked in accordance with the levels-based mark scheme on pages 61.

⭐ Make sure your answer to this question is in paragraphs and full sentences. Bullet points have been used in this example answer to suggest some information you could include. There are four marks available for spelling, punctuation and grammar, so make sure you read through your answer carefully, correcting any mistakes.

THEMES: APPEARANCE AND REALITY

Shakespeare uses the theme of appearance and reality to warn the audience that deception eventually leads to a person's downfall.

The Witches

The Witches use antithesis in the opening scene to suggest that not everything is as it seems. In Act 1, Scene 1, the line: "*Fair is foul, and foul is fair*" sets the tone for the whole play, and the Witches' deliberately ambiguous language drives Macbeth's actions.

> **Comment:** The line "*Fair is foul*" refers to the Macbeths who outwardly appear "*fair*" but are inwardly "*foul*". The line "*foul is fair*" could reference the characters who are wrongly accused of murder. For example, Malcolm is suspected of arranging his father's death, but he is eventually proven to be innocent.
>
> Although the Witches use misleading language to deceive Macbeth, they don't pretend to be something they're not. They are presented as evil, wicked and vindictive, and they stay true to that characterisation throughout the play.

Macbeth

Initially, the other characters believe Macbeth to be a loyal and brave man, but the audience realises that this outward appearance is false. In reality, he is deceitful and weak.

> **Comment:** The audience recognises Macbeth's true nature before the other characters do. This creates dramatic irony. The audience knows that Macbeth cannot be trusted, yet they must watch as characters are repeatedly deceived by him.

Macbeth initially attempts to mask his true nature. He frames Duncan's servants for the murder in order to hide his own guilt. However, as the play progresses, Macbeth cares less and less about disguising his true nature. He doesn't attempt to frame anyone for the murder of the Macduffs, and eventually the other characters recognise he is a "*tyrant*". When the thanes realise Macbeth's true character, they abandon him and switch allegiance to Malcolm and Macduff.

Macbeth is able to deceive the other characters at first

> **Comment:** Shakespeare uses the theme of appearance and reality to explore that you can never be certain who to trust and that outward appearances can be deceptive. Shakespeare also suggests that people cannot hide their true nature forever.

Lady Macbeth

Lady Macbeth is ambitious and power-hungry, but she cleverly disguises her intentions and deceives the other characters. For example, outwardly, Lady Macbeth appears loyal to King Duncan. She graciously welcomes him into her home, and flatters him: *"For those of old, / And the late dignities heaped up to them, / We rest your hermits."* However, she is secretly plotting to betray Duncan to achieve her ambitions.

This painting shows Lady Macbeth examining her hands from Act 5, Scene 1

Comment: Lady Macbeth tells her husband: *"Look like th' innocent flower, / But be the serpent under 't."* She stresses the importance of faking their outward appearances to disguise their true intentions. Serpents are often linked to the biblical story of Adam and Eve, where the snake tricks Eve and brings about the fall of man, so snakes are often associated with deception and the devil.

Lady Macbeth uses her femininity to deceive the other characters. As a woman, she is assumed to be weak and subservient. However, she repeatedly dominates Macbeth, by taunting and bullying him.

Ultimately, Lady Macbeth's deceit brings about her downfall. She is driven mad by her guilt and hallucinations.

Comment: Lady Macbeth's hallucinations are ironic. She tried to deceive others by manipulating reality, but eventually her downfall is caused by her own mind manipulating reality.

The supernatural

The ghostly dagger in Act 2, Scene 1 and the ghost of Banquo in Act 3, Scene 4 also symbolise appearance and reality. It's not clear whether either of these visions are real, or just Macbeth hallucinating. The line between reality and deception has become blurred, so the audience is unsure what is real and what is not, just like Macbeth.

THEMES: KINGSHIP

When *Macbeth* was written, King James had only recently become King of England, and English people were keen to see what kind of ruler he would be. The topic of kingship would have been very relevant to audiences in 1606.

Good kings

Duncan

Duncan is presented positively. He is noble, grateful and generous, rewarding his loyal thanes with land and titles. He is also described as "*a most sainted king*" which reinforces the idea that kings were appointed by God (see **page 3** for more on the Divine Right of Kings). Even Macbeth admires Duncan's leadership: "*So clear in his great office.*"

Comment: Duncan is presented as an ideal king. This contrasts with Macbeth's tyrannical rule, and emphasises what a poor leader Macbeth is.

However, Duncan is naïve as he is betrayed by the Thane of Cawdor. Duncan doesn't learn from his mistakes, and this trusting nature is also exploited by the Macbeths. Shakespeare suggests that being too kind-hearted is a negative attribute for kings.

Comment: Duncan's death brings with it a terrible storm, which suggests that God is appalled by his murder and the disruption of the Divine Right of Kings.

Good kings continued

Malcolm

Malcolm is Duncan's son, and is named as next in line to the throne when he is given the title of Prince of Cumberland in Act 1, Scene 4. This establishes Malcolm as the rightful heir of Scotland.

Comment: Producing an heir was considered an important part of being a king because it would ensure the stability of the country after the king's death by avoiding multiple claimants to the throne and the threat of civil war.

When Duncan is murdered, Malcolm flees to England. This could be interpreted as cowardice, suggesting that Malcolm isn't prepared to avenge his father and claim what is rightfully his. However, Malcolm's escape implies that he has learned from his father's mistakes about trusting the wrong people, which suggests he will be a wiser king than his father. This cautious nature is shown again in Act 4, Scene 3, where he tests Macduff's loyalty before confiding in him.

In Act 4, Scene 3, Malcolm discusses his qualities: he's loyal, honest and selfless, and he puts his country before himself: *"What I am truly, / Is thine and my poor country's to command."* Malcolm's attributes suggest he is the opposite of Macbeth, implying that he will be a good king.

Comment: The desire to be king drives the actions of both Malcolm and Macbeth, but for very different reasons. Macbeth wants to be king due to his own selfish ambition, whereas Malcolm wants to be king to put an end to Macbeth's tyranny.

When Macbeth is defeated and Malcolm becomes king, he rewards the thanes: *"Henceforth be earls."* This suggests that he will be just as grateful and generous as his father.

Symbolism — kingship and nature

Shakespeare uses imagery of planting and growing to symbolise being nurtured by a good king. In Act 1, Scene 4, Duncan tells Banquo: *"I have begun to plant thee, and will labour / To make thee full of growing."* Banquo responds *"There, if I grow, / The harvest is your own."* In Act 5, Scene 8 after defeating Macbeth, Malcolm tells the thanes: *"What's more to do, / Which would be planted newly with the time"*. The semantic field of nature has connotations of new life which brings hope, but also contrasts with the imagery of death associated with Macbeth, who is described as a *"butcher"*.

Good kings continued

King Edward

In Act 3, Scene 6, King Edward of England is described as "*holy*", "*saintly*" and "*pious*", implying that strong religious beliefs were considered a good attribute for a monarch. This is reinforced in Act 4, Scene 3, where a doctor tells Malcolm that King Edward can cure the sick with his touch. This ability to perform miracles is believed to be a gift from God, which emphasises the belief in the Divine Right of Kings (see **page 3**).

Comment: King Edward is a reference to a real English King, Edward the Confessor, who ruled between 1042–1066. He was made a saint in 1161. Like Duncan, Edward's goodness contrasts with Macbeth's wickedness.

Bad kings

Macbeth

Before Macbeth murders Duncan, he seems to possess qualities that would have made him a good king. He's brave, and he "*wouldst not play false*", suggesting that he is honourable.

However, when Macbeth becomes king he is corrupted by power, and abuses his position which results in terrible things happening to Scotland. Under Macbeth's rule, Scotland is personified as a woman who "*weeps, it bleeds, and each new day a gash / Is added to her wounds.*" Macbeth's ambition to become king has thrown the country into chaos where "*Each new morn / New widows howl, new orphans cry.*"

Terrible things happen to Scotland when Macbeth becomes king.

Comment: Shakespeare explores the impact that a poor ruler can have on a country.

Macbeth doesn't have an heir, and this makes him resent Banquo and the prophecy of Banquo's descendants becoming kings.

EXAMINATION PRACTICE

Read this extract from Act 2, Scene 2. At this point in the play, Macbeth has just murdered Duncan, but he has forgotten to plant the daggers next to Duncan's sleeping servants.

MACBETH

> I'll go no more:
> I am afraid to think what I have done;
> Look on 't again I dare not.

LADY MACBETH

> Infirm of purpose!
> Give me the daggers. The sleeping and the dead
> Are but as pictures. 'Tis the eye of childhood
> That fears a painted devil. If he do bleed,
> I'll gild the faces of the grooms withal,
> For it must seem their guilt.

LADY MACBETH exits

A knock sounds offstage

MACBETH

> Whence is that knocking?
> How is 't with me when every noise appals me?
> What hands are here? Ha! They pluck out mine eyes.
> Will all great Neptune's ocean wash this blood
> Clean from my hand? No, this my hand will rather
> The multitudinous seas incarnadine,
> Making the green one red.

Starting with this point in the play, explore how Shakespeare presents the attitudes of Macbeth and Lady Macbeth towards guilt.
- How Shakespeare presents the attitudes of Macbeth and Lady Macbeth towards guilt in this extract
- How far Shakespeare presents the attitudes of Macbeth and Lady Macbeth towards guilt in the play as a whole.

[30 + 4]

EXAMINATION PRACTICE ANSWERS

In this extract, Shakespeare presents Macbeth's guilt through fear. Macbeth refuses to return to the scene of Duncan's murder to plant the daggers on the sleeping servants: "*Look on 't again I dare not.*" This is not the first time that Macbeth has killed a man, as there were reports in Act 1, Scene 2 that he killed men in battle, but Macbeth's guilt over Duncan's murder has transformed him from a heroic warrior, into a fearful, paranoid man. Macbeth uses imagery of washing his hands in "*great Neptune's ocean*" to show the magnitude of his guilt; he feels so guilty he would turn "*The multitudinous seas incarnadine*" [red]. Throughout the play, references to handwashing symbolise guilt, and this reference foreshadows Lady Macbeth's handwashing in Act 5. Macbeth's language also presents his guilty and tormented state of mind. The repetition of rhetorical questions such as "*What hands are here?*" imply that he is confused and disturbed by Duncan's death. The act of regicide would have been very shocking to 17th century audiences, especially with the regard to the Divine Right of Kings, whereby it was believed that kings were chosen by God. As such, killing a king would have been interpreted as a direct attack on God.

Contrastingly, Lady Macbeth shows no remorse in this extract. Rather than feeling guilt for Duncan's death, she's angry that Macbeth has forgotten to frame the servants and she chides him for it: "*Infirm of purpose!*" She is the one who returns to Duncan's room to finish the job. She calmly remarks that corpses are "*but as pictures*", showing that she has detached any humanity from Duncan's body, which suggests her indifference and lack of guilt. Lady Macbeth's lack of remorse in this scene would have been shocking to 17th century audiences, who would have expected women to be the weaker, gentler sex, but here, Lady Macbeth is the more fearless of the two.

In Act 3, Macbeth and Lady Macbeth both shows signs of remorse. Lady Macbeth remarks that they "*dwell in doubtful joy*" and Macbeth tells her that it is "*Better be with the dead.*" Although Macbeth is initially plagued by guilt, it doesn't stop him from committing crimes, showing that he is prepared to endure guilt to achieve his ambitions. He orders three men to kill Banquo, and after the murder has been committed, Macbeth's guilt manifests as the ghost of Banquo. Banquo is the only character who appears as a ghost, suggesting that Macbeth feels especially guilty for this crime. However, by Act 5, Macbeth and Lady Macbeth's attitudes towards guilt are entirely reversed. Lady Macbeth has been driven mad by guilt, as shown by her sleepwalking and incessant handwashing, to the point that she kills herself. Macbeth on the other hand, becomes indifferent towards his actions, and shows no remorse for the atrocities he has committed, such as slaughtering the Macduffs.

LEVELS-BASED MARK SCHEMES FOR EXTENDED RESPONSE QUESTIONS

Questions that require extended writing use mark bands. The whole answer will be marked together to determine which mark band it fits into and which mark should be awarded within the mark band.

The descriptors have been written in simple language to give an indication of the expectations of each mark band. See the AQA website for the official mark schemes used.

Level	Students' answers tend to...
6 (26–30 marks)	- Focus on the text as conscious construct (i.e. a play written by Shakespeare intended to have a deliberate effect). - Produce a logical and well-structured response which closely uses the text to explore their argument / interpretation. - Analyse the writer's craft by considering the effects of a writer's choice, linked closely to meanings. - Understand the writer's purpose and context.
5 (21–25 marks)	- Start to think about ideas in a more developed way. - Think about the deeper meaning of a text and start to explore alternative interpretations. - Start to focus on specific elements of writer's craft, linked to meanings. - Focus more on abstract concepts, such as themes and ideas, than narrative events or character feelings.
4 (16–20 marks)	- Sustain a focus on an idea, or a particular technique. - Start to consider how the text works and what the writer is doing. - Use examples effectively to support their points. - Explain the effect of a writer's method on the text, with a clear focus on it having been consciously written. - Show an understanding of ideas and themes.
3 (11–15 marks)	- Explain their ideas. - Demonstrate knowledge of the text as a whole. - Show awareness of the concept of themes. - Identify the effects of a range of methods on reader.
2 (6–10 marks)	- Support their comments by using references to / from the text. - Make comments that are generally relevant to the question. - Identify at least one method and possibly make some comment on the effect of it on the reader.
1 (1–5 marks)	- Describe the text. - Retell the narrative. - Make references to, rather than use references from, the text.
0 marks	Nothing worthy of credit / nothing written.

INDEX

A
acts 6
ambition 14, 16, 47
Angus 15, 16, 30
antagonist 2, 45
antithesis 11–13, 44, 54
apostrophes 7
apparition 26, 27, 30, 45, 46, 51
appearance and reality 11, 12, 16, 54
Assessment Objectives vi

B
Banquo 3, 11, 13–16, 18, 22, 23, 42, 47
bear-baiting 32
Birnam Wood 27, 30, 31, 35
blank verse 8
bloodied captain 12
bloody hands 10, 11, 19, 30

C
catharsis 2
comic relief 20
context 3
cyclical structure 4

D
Daemonologie 4, 50
Divine Right of Kings 3, 19, 21
Donalbain 11, 12, 15, 16, 21, 46
dramatic irony 6, 11, 13, 15, 16, 28, 54
Duncan 11–13, 15–17, 19, 23, 43, 56
Dunsinane Hill 27, 30

E
equivocation 4

F
fatal flaw 2, 47
fate 22, 23
femininity 5, 55
Fife 21
Fleance 18, 22, 23, 34
foil 11, 18, 42
foreshadowing 10, 11, 12, 19, 20

G
gender roles 5
ghostly dagger 18, 51, 55
ghost of Banquo 24, 34, 42, 51, 55
guilt 19, 30, 39
Gunpowder Plot 4
Guy Fawkes 4

H
handwashing 19, 29
Hecate 25, 44, 50

I
iambic pentameter 8
imagery 11, 23
Inverness 15

K
King Edward 28, 58
King James I 3, 4, 28, 42, 50, 56
kingship 17, 56

L
Lady Macbeth 5, 16–19, 21–24, 29, 31, 33, 38, 39, 47, 55
Lady Macduff 27
Lennox 10, 12, 15, 16, 20–22, 25, 27, 30
line numbers 6

M
Macbeth 13–15, 17–24, 26, 30–35, 47, 54, 58
Macdonald 12
Macduff 5, 16, 20, 21, 25–28, 30–32, 45
Malcolm 5, 12, 15, 16, 21, 27, 28, 30–32, 46, 57
masculinity 5, 22, 24
murderers 22, 24, 27

O
Old Man 21
Old Siward 32

P
pace 29
patriarchal society 5
porter 4, 9, 20
prince of Cumberland 15
pronouns 7
prophecy 14, 18, 16, 30, 32, 33
prose 9
protagonist 2, 33
puns 11

R

regicide 3, 18
religion 3
rhyming couplets 9, 12, 23
rhythm 8
Ross 13–16, 21, 22, 27, 28

S

satire 4
scenes 6
Scone 21
sentence order 8
setting 3, 6
Seyton 31
Shakespeare 2
Shakespeare's Globe 6
shared lines 8
sleepwalking 10, 29, 30, 39
soliloquy 9, 10, 16–18, 22, 33
stage directions 6
stressed syllables 8
supernatural 4, 12, 16, 18, 24, 50
symbolism 10, 57

T

Thane of Cawdor 12–15
Thane of Glamis 2
theatre 5
The King's Men 3
tragedies 2
trochaic tetrameter 9, 44

U

unstressed syllables 8

V

verbs 7
verse 8

W

witchcraft 4, 50
Witches 9, 12–14, 18, 20, 23–27, 44, 50, 54
witch hunts 4

Y

Young Siward 32

ACKNOWLEDGMENTS

The questions in the ClearRevise textbook are the sole responsibility of the authors and have neither been provided nor approved by the examination board.

Every effort has been made to trace and acknowledge ownership of copyright. The publishers will be happy to make any future amendments with copyright owners that it has not been possible to contact. The publisher would like to thank the following companies and individuals who granted permission for the use of their images in this textbook.

Page 2 — Shakespeare © Nicku / Shutterstock

Page 3 — King James I © Everett Collection / Shutterstock

Page 4 — Witchcraft: a white-faced witch meeting a black-faced witch with a great beast. Woodcut, 1720. Wellcome Collection.

Page 5 — © Donald Cooper / Alamy Stock Photo. Kate Fleetwood (Lady Macbeth), Patrick Stewart (Macbeth) in MACBETH by Shakespeare at the Minerva Theatre, Chichester Festival Theatre.

Page 5 — Globe theatre © Nick Brundle Photography / Shutterstock

Page 6 — Globe theatre © RichartPhotos / Shutterstock

Page 8 — © Imageplotter / Alamy Live News. Harry Anton and Helen Millar take on the roles of Macbeth and Lady Macbeth.

Page 9 — An episode in Macbeth by William Shakespeare: the three witches. Mezzotint by J.R. Smith, 1785, after Johann Heinrich Füssli, 1783. Wellcome Collection.

Page 12 — © theatrepix / Alamy Stock Photo. Terence Keeley as Bloody Captain and Nadia Albina, Danielle Bird, Scarlett Brookes and Kerry Gooderson as Wyrd Sisters.

Page 18 — © theatrepix / Alamy Stock Photo. Ray Fearon and Tara Fitzgerald.

Page 22 — © theatrepix / Alamy Stock Photo. Ray Fearon and Tara Fitzgerald.

Page 29 — © IanDagnall Computing / Alamy Stock Photo. Lady Macbeth Sleepwalking by Henry Fuseli (Johann Heinrich Füssli; 1741-1825), c.1784.

Page 33 — © See Saw Films / Album / Alamy Stock Photo.

Page 35 — © Everett Collection Inc / Alamy Stock Photo. Michael Fassbender, Macbeth, 2015

Page 38 — © Everett Collection Inc / Alamy Stock Photo. Macbeth, Marion Cotillard as Lady Macbeth, 2015. © The Weinstein Company / courtesy Everett Collection

Page 42 — © Moviestore Collection Ltd / Alamy Stock Photo. Macbeth (poster) (2015) Paddy Considine Justin Kurzel (Dir) Moviestore Collection Ltd

Page 43 — Duncan, Macduff © Tim_Booth / Shutterstock

Page 44 — © Everett Collection Inc / Alamy Stock Photo. Macbeth, The Three Witches, 1954 TV production released theatrically

Page 47 — © theatrepix / Alamy Stock Photo. Ray Fearon and Tara Fitzgerald.

page 50 — © Chronicle / Alamy Stock Photo. Title-page of 'Daemonologie' by King James VI of Scotland (James I of England) Date: 1597

Page 51 — © Donald Cooper / Alamy Stock Photo. Ian McKellen (Macbeth) in Macbeth by Shakespeare directed by Trevor Nunn for the Royal Shakespeare Company (RSC) in Stratford-upon-Avon in 1976.

Page 54 — © theatrepix / Alamy Stock Photo. Ray Fearon (Macbeth)

Page 55 — © History and Art Collection / Alamy Stock Photo. Lady Macbeth by Alfred Stevens

Page 58 — © Allstar Picture Library Limited. / Alamy Stock Photo. Jon Finch, Macbeth, 1971

All other photos and graphics © Shutterstock.

EXAMINATION TIPS

With your examination practice, use a boundary approximation using the following table. Be aware that the grade boundaries can vary from year to year, so they should be used as a guide only.

Grade	9	8	7	6	5	4	3	2	1
Boundary	88%	79%	71%	61%	52%	43%	31%	21%	10%

1. Read the question carefully. Don't give an answer to a question that you think is appearing (or wish was appearing!) rather than the actual question.
2. Spend time reading through the extract, and think about what happens before and after, and how it links to other parts of the play. The statement above the extract will help you identify where in the play it is from.
3. It's worth jotting down a quick plan to make sure your answer includes sufficient detail and is focused on the question.
4. The question will ask you about the extract and the play as a whole, but you don't need to spend an equal amount of time on both. If you're struggling to make close textual references about the extract, you can concentrate on the rest of the play instead.
5. A discussion of Shakespeare's methods can include his language choices, but also structural choices (such as the ordering of events), how characters develop, and what their actions tell you about their characterisation.
6. Include details from the text to support your answer. These details might be quotes, or they can be references to the text. Don't worry if you can't remember quotes from other parts of the play. You will be marked on the strength of your answer to the question, not the accuracy of your quotations.
7. Make sure your handwriting is legible. The examiner can't award you marks if they can't read what you've written.
8. The examiner will be impressed if you can correctly use technical terms like 'foil', 'soliloquy', 'iambic pentameter', 'rhyming couplets' but to be awarded the best marks, you need to explore the effect of these techniques.
9. Use linking words and phrases to show you are developing your points or comparing information, for example, "this reinforces", "this shows that" and "on the other hand". This helps to give your answer structure, and makes it easier for the examiner to award you marks.
10. If you need extra paper, make sure you clearly signal that your answer is continued elsewhere. Remember that longer answers don't necessarily score more highly than shorter, more concise answers.
11. There are 4 marks available for spelling, punctuation and grammar. Save some time at the end of the exam to read through your answer and correct any mistakes.

Good luck!

New titles coming soon!

Revision, re-imagined

These guides are everything you need to ace your exams and beam with pride. Each topic is laid out in a beautifully illustrated format that is clear, approachable and as concise and simple as possible.

They have been expertly compiled and edited by subject specialists, highly experienced examiners, industry professionals and a good dollop of scientific research into what makes revision most effective. Past examination questions are essential to good preparation, improving understanding and confidence.

- Hundreds of marks worth of examination style questions
- Answers provided for all questions within the books
- Illustrated topics to improve memory and recall
- Specification references for every topic
- Examination tips and techniques
- Free Python solutions pack (CS Only)

Absolute clarity is the aim.

Explore the series and add to your collection at **www.clearrevise.com**

Available from all good book shops

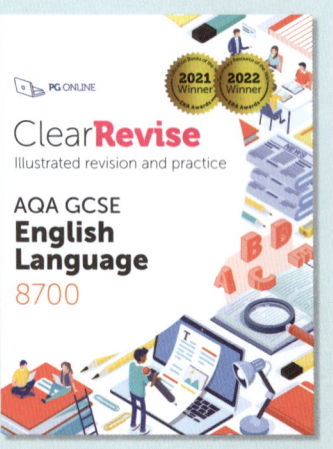

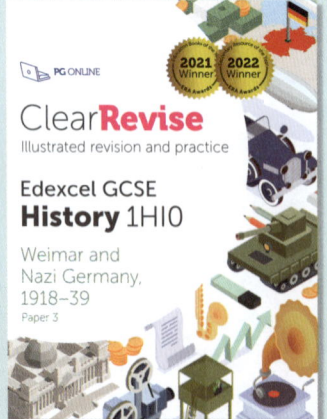

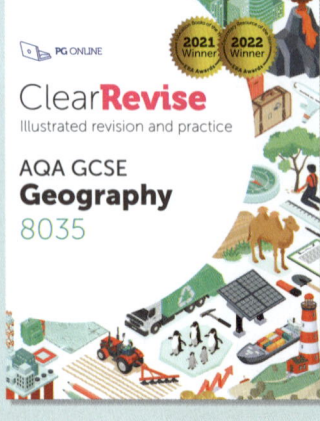

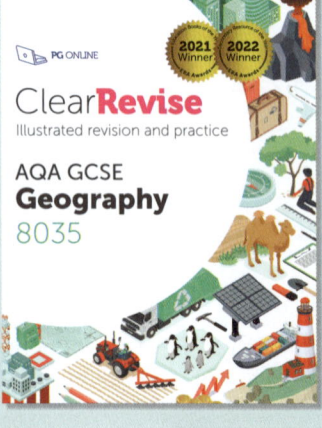

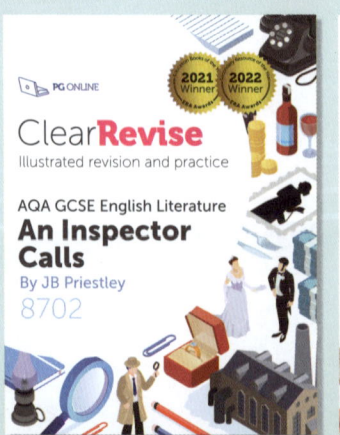

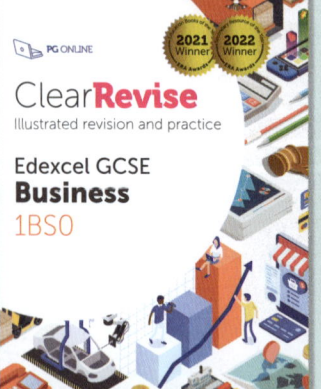

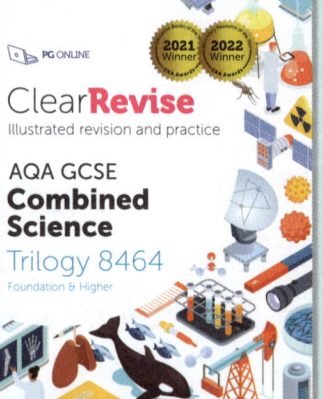

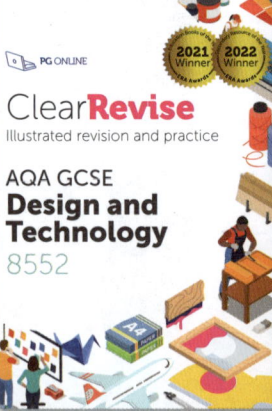

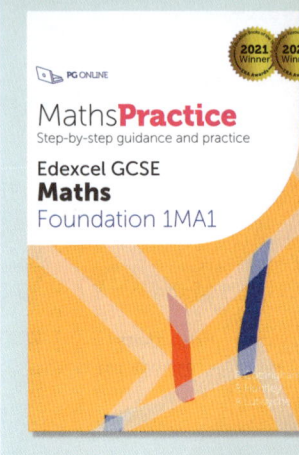

amazon   @pgonlinepub

MathsPractice
Step-by-step guidance and practice
Edexcel GCSE
Maths
Foundation 1MA1

ClearRevise
Illustrated revision and practice
OCR
Creative iMedia
Levels 1/2
J834 (R093, R094)

ClearRevise
Illustrated revision and practice
AQA GCSE
English Language
8700

ClearRevise
Illustrated revision and practice
Edexcel GCSE
History 1HI0
Weimar and Nazi Germany, 1918–39
Paper 3

ClearRevise
Illustrated revision and practice
AQA GCSE
Geography
8035

ClearRevise
Illustrated revision and practice
OCR GCSE
Computer Science
J277

ClearRevise
Illustrated revision and practice
AQA GCSE English Literature
An Inspector Calls
By JB Priestley
8702

ClearRevise
Illustrated revision and practice
Edexcel GCSE
Business
1BS0

ClearRevise
Illustrated revision and practice
AQA GCSE
Combined Science
Trilogy 8464
Foundation & Higher

ClearRevise
Illustrated revision and practice
AQA GCSE
Design and Technology
8552